Windows Vista™ Just the Steps™ FOR DUMMIES®

by Nancy Muir

BICENTENNIAL
1807
WILEY
2007
BICENTENNIAL

Wiley Publishing, Inc.

Windows Vista™ Just the Steps™ For Dummies®

Published by
Wiley Publishing, Inc.
111 River Street
Hoboken, NJ 07030-5774
www.wiley.com

Copyright © 2007 by Wiley Publishing, Inc., Indianapolis, Indiana

Published by Wiley Publishing, Inc., Indianapolis, Indiana

Published simultaneously in Canada

For general information on our other products and services, please contact our Customer Care Department within the U.S. at 800-762-2974, outside the U.S. at 317-572-3993, or fax 317-572-4002.

For technical support, please visit www.wiley.com/techsupport.

Wiley also publishes its books in a variety of electronic formats. Some content that appears in print may not be available in electronic books.

Library of Congress Control Number: 2006936744

ISBN: 978-0-471-78685-6

Manufactured in the United States of America

10 9 8 7 6 5 4 3 2

1B/SY/QS/QX/IN

WILEY

About the Author

Nancy Muir has written over 50 books on topics ranging from desktop applications to online safety and distance learning. She has also contributed articles to several national magazines on topics such as distance learning and home design. Prior to her freelance career, Nancy worked in the software and book publishing industries and has taught technical writing at the university level. She holds a certificate in distance learning design.

Dedication

To my wonderful husband, Earl, for his neverending support and love. And to his folks, Nettie and Dick, for putting up with my hectic schedule during their summer visit with grace and humor.

Author's Acknowledgments

The author would like to thank the folks at Wiley for their continued faith in her work, and specifically Kyle Looper and Blair Pottenger, the acquisitions and project editors on this book, respectively. Their support and encouragement made working on a tight schedule with a very new version of Windows bearable!

Publisher's Acknowledgments

We're proud of this book; please send us your comments through our online registration form located at www.dummies.com/register/. Some of the people who helped bring this book to market include the following:

Acquisitions, Editorial, and Media Development

Project Editor: Blair J. Pottenger

Acquisitions Editor: Kyle Looper

Senior Copy Editor: Teresa Artman

Technical Editor: Lee Musick

Editorial Manager: Kevin Kirschner

Media Development Specialists: Angela Denny, Kate Jenkins, Steven Kudirka, Kit Malone

Media Development Manager: Laura VanWinkle

Editorial Assistant: Amanda Foxworth

Sr. Editorial Assistant: Cherie Case

Cartoons: Rich Tennant (www.the5thwave.com)

Composition Services

Project Coordinator: Jennifer Theriot

Layout and Graphics: Denny Hager, Heather Ryan, Ronald Terry, Erin Zeltner

Proofreaders: Linda Seifert, Charles Spencer, Brian H. Walls

Indexer: Lynnzee Elze

Publishing and Editorial for Technology Dummies

Richard Swadley, Vice President and Executive Group Publisher

Andy Cummings, Vice President and Publisher

Mary Bednarek, Executive Acquisitions Director

Mary C. Corder, Editorial Director

Publishing for Consumer Dummies

Diane Graves Steele, Vice President and Publisher

Joyce Pepple, Acquisitions Director

Composition Services

Gerry Fahey, Vice President of Production Services

Debbie Stailey, Director of Composition Services

Contents at a Glance

I'm guessing you have a healthy dislike of computer books. You don't want to wade through a long tome on Windows Vista. Rather, you just want to get in, find out how to do something, and get out. You're not alone. I was itching to write a book where I could get right to the details of how to do things — and move on. None of that telling you what I'm going to tell you, saying my piece, and then reviewing for you what I just said. That's why I was delighted to tackle a *Just the Steps For Dummies* book on Windows Vista.

About This Book

Windows Vista is a very robust piece of software, with about as much functionality as Einstein on a good day. If you own a Windows Vista computer (and I assume you do, or you should rush back to the bookstore for a refund, pronto!) you likely spend a lot of time everyday in the Windows Vista environment. Knowing how to harness the power of this operating system is what this book is all about. As the title suggests, I give you just the steps you need to do many of the most common Windows Vista tasks. This book is all about getting productive right away.

Why You Need This Book

You can't wait weeks to master Windows Vista. It's where all your software lives as well as how you get to your e-mail and documents. You have to figure out Windows Vista quickly. You might need to poke around Windows Vista and do work while learning. When you hit a bump in the road, you need a quick answer to get you moving again. This book is full of quick, clear steps that keep your learning in high gear.

Introduction

Conventions used in this book

➡ When you have to type something in a text box, I put it in **bold** type.

➡ For menu commands, I use the ⇨ symbol to separate menu items. For example, choose Tools⇨Internet Options. The ⇨ symbol is just my way of saying "Choose Internet Options from the Tools menu."

➡ Points of interest in some figures are circled. The text tells you what to look for, and the circle makes it easy to find.

 This icon points out insights or helpful suggestions related to tasks in the step list.

How This Book Is Organized

This book is conveniently divided into several handy parts.

Part I: Working in Windows Vista

Here's where you get the basics of opening and closing software applications, working with files and folders to manage the documents you create, and using built-in Windows applications like the Calculator and WordPad.

Part II: Getting on the Internet

The whole world is online, and you can't be left behind. Here's where I show you how to connect, how to browse, ways for using the Internet to stay in touch when you're on the road, and how to do e-mail.

Part III: Setting Up Hardware and Networks

In addition to software, Windows helps you work with hardware and connections between computers. You might have to make a little effort to set up new hardware or a home network. This part is where I show you how to do that.

Part IV: Customizing the Windows Desktop

You want Windows Vista to function in a way that matches your style, right? This is the part where I cover customizing the look of Windows Vista, customizing its behavior, and making it user friendly for those with access challenges.

Part V: Using Security and Maintenance Features

Windows Vista provides lots of ways to keep your information safe, from passwords to protect your files to tools to prevent viruses and spyware from attacking your system. There are also several features that help keep your system up to date and trouble-free.

Part VI: Fixing Common Problems

Yes, I admit it, even Windows Vista can have problems. Luckily, it also has tools to get you out of trouble. In this part, I explain how to deal with hardware and software problems as well as how to get help when you need it.

Part VII: Fun and Games

Finally, you've earned some fun. Go to these chapters to discover a world of games, music, and photos just waiting for you in Windows Vista.

Get Ready To . . .

Whether you need to open a piece of software and get working, check your e-mail, or get online, just browse this book, pick a task, and jump in. Windows Vista can be your best friend if you know how to use it, and the tasks covered in this book will make you a Windows Vista master in no time.

Part I
Working in Windows Vista

The 5th Wave   By Rich Tennant

UBER-USER DWAYNE GRANTZ CHALKS UP BEFORE PUTTING WINDOWS VISTA THROUGH ITS PACES.

Exploring the Windows Vista Desktop

*J*ust as your desk is the central area from which you do all kinds of work, the Windows Vista desktop is a command center for organizing your computer work. Here you find the Start menu, which you use to access information about your computer, files, folders, and applications. You'll also find a taskbar that offers settings, such as your computer's date and time, as well as shortcuts to your most frequently accessed programs or files.

In this chapter, you explore the desktop, which appears when you log on to Windows Vista. Along the way, you discover the Recycle Bin, the Quick Launch bar (this might sound like a salad bar at a fast-food restaurant, but it's actually the area of the Windows Vista taskbar that lets you open frequently used programs), and how to shut down your computer when you're done for the day.

Here, then, are the procedures that you can use to take advantage of the desktop features of Windows Vista.

Log On and Off Windows Vista

1. Turn on your computer to begin the Windows Vista start-up sequence.

2. In the resulting Windows Vista Welcome screen, enter your password and click the arrow button (or click Switch User and choose another user to log on as). Windows Vista verifies your password and displays the Windows Vista desktop, as shown in Figure 1-1. (*Note:* If you haven't set up the password protection feature or more than one user, you're taken directly to the Windows Vista desktop. For more on adding and changing passwords, see Chapter 12.)

3. To log off the current user account, first save any open documents, close any open applications, and then choose Start. Then click the arrow next to the Lock button and choose Log Off. Windows Vista logs off and displays a list of users. To log on again, click a user icon.

 To create another user, choose Start↔Control Panel↔User Accounts and Family Safety↔Add or Remove User Accounts. Then click Create a New Account. Follow instructions to enter a name for the account and set a password for it, if you like.

 To log on as another user as described in Step 3, you have to enable Fast User Switching in the User Account settings.

Figure 1-1: The Windows Vista desktop

 After you set up more than one user, before you get to the password screen, you have to click the icon for the user you wish to log on as.

Work with the Start Menu

1. Press the Windows key on your keyboard or click the Start button on the desktop to display the Start menu (see Figure 1-2).

2. From the Start menu, you can do any of the following:

   • Click All Programs to display a list of all programs on your computer. You can click any program in the list to open it.

   • Click any category on the right of the Start menu to display a Windows Explorer window with related folders and files (see Figure 1-3).

   • Click either frequently used programs at the top left of the Start menu or recently used programs just below them.

   • Click the Power button icon to close all programs and turn off Windows, or click the Lock icon to lock your computer.

   • Click the arrow next to the Lock button to display a menu of choices for shutting down or restarting your computer, logging off, or for logging in as a different user.

3. When you move your cursor away from the Start menu, it disappears.

 Open the Start menu and right-click in a blank area, and click Properties to display the Taskbar and Start Menu Properties dialog box, where you can customize the Start menu behavior. If you would rather use the look and feel of the Start menu in older versions of Windows, select Classic Start Menu in the Taskbar and Start Menu Properties dialog box and then click OK.

Figure 1-2: The Start menu

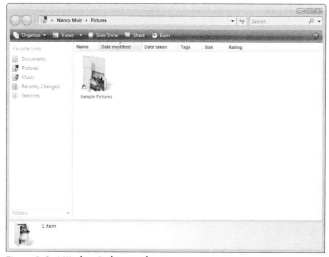

Figure 1-3: A Windows Explorer window

Work with the Quick Launch Bar

1. Locate the Quick Launch bar on the taskbar just to the right of the Start button; if it's not visible, right-click the taskbar and choose Toolbars⇨Quick Launch from the shortcut menu (see Figure 1-4). By default, it includes the Show Desktop and Switch between Windows icons.

2. To place any application on the Quick Launch bar, as shown in Figure 1-5, right-click that application in the Start menu or on the Desktop and then choose Add to Quick Launch. You can also click and drag it to the Quick Launch bar. (If you want help creating a desktop shortcut, see the task, "Create a Desktop Shortcut," later in this chapter.)

 If you have more programs in this area than can be shown on the taskbar, click the arrows to the right of the Quick Launch bar; a shortcut menu of programs appears. However, don't create too much clutter on your Quick Launch bar, which can make it unwieldy. Logical candidates to place here are your Internet browser, your e-mail program, and programs that you use every day, such as a word processor or calendar program.

 When the Quick Launch bar is displayed, the Show Desktop button is available. When you click this button, all open applications are reduced to taskbar icons. It's a quick way to clean your desktop — or hide what you're up to!

Figure 1-4: The Toolbars menu

Figure 1-5: Add icons to the Quick Launch bar

Set the Date and Time

1. Press the Windows key on your keyboard to display the taskbar if it isn't visible.

2. Right-click the Date/Time display on the far right of the taskbar and then choose Adjust Date/Time from the shortcut menu that appears.

3. Click the Change Date and Time (see Figure 1-6) button and in the Date and Time Settings dialog box click another date on the calendar. Enter a new time in the Time box to change the time. Click OK.

4. To change the time zone, from the Date and Time Properties dialog box click the Change Time Zone button. Choose another time zone from the Time Zone list and click OK.

5. Click OK to apply the new settings and close the dialog box.

 If you don't want your computer to adjust for Daylight Saving Time, click Change Time Zone and click the Automatically Adjust Clock for Daylight Saving Time checkbox to turn this feature off.

 Another option for displaying the time or date is to add the Clock or Calendar gadgets to the Windows Sidebar. You can also drag gadgets right onto your desktop if you prefer not to leave the Sidebar displayed. See Chapter 5 for more about using the Sidebar and Gadgets.

Figure 1-6: The Date and Time Properties dialog box

Arrange Icons on the Desktop

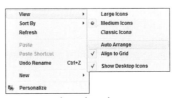

1. Right-click the desktop and choose View in the resulting shortcut menu; be sure that Auto Arrange isn't selected, as shown in Figure 1-7. (If it is selected, deselect it before proceeding to the next step.)

2. Right-click the Windows Vista desktop. In the resulting shortcut menu, choose Sort By and then click the criteria for sorting your desktop shortcuts (see Figure 1-8).

3. You can also click any icon and drag it to another location on the desktop — for example, to separate it from other desktop icons so you can find it easily.

Figure 1-7: The Desktop shortcut menu, View submenu

Figure 1-8: The Desktop shortcut menu, Sort By submenu

 If you've rearranged your desktop by moving items hither, thither, and yon and you want your icons in orderly rows along the left side of your desktop, snap them into place with the Auto Arrange feature. Right-click the desktop and then choose View⇨Auto Arrange.

 Want to quickly hide all your desktop open windows? Say the boss is headed your way, and all you have there is games? Click the Show Desktop icon on the Quick Launch bar. Poof! They're all gone, and your job is secure. Just click items on the taskbar to display each window again.

Create a Desktop Shortcut

1. Choose Start⇨All Programs and locate the program on the list of programs that appears.

2. Right-click an item, Freecell for example, and choose Send To⇨Desktop (Create Shortcut) (see Figure 1-9).

3. The shortcut appears on the desktop (see Figure 1-10). Double-click the icon to open the application.

Occasionally, Windows Vista offers to delete desktop icons that you haven't used in a long time. Let it. The desktop should be reserved for frequently used programs, files, and folders. You can always re-create shortcuts easily if you need them again.

To clean up your desktop manually, right-click the desktop and choose Personalize. Click Change Desktop Icons in the Tasks list on the left. In the Desktop Icons setting dialog box that appears, click the Restore Default button, which returns to the original desktop shortcuts set up on your computer.

You can create a shortcut for a brand new item by right-clicking the desktop, choosing New, and then choosing an item to place there, such as a text document, bitmap image, or contact. Then double-click the shortcut that appears and begin working on the file in the associated application.

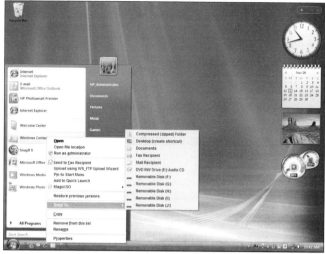

Figure 1-9: The Send To shortcut menu

Figure 1-10: A new shortcut on the desktop

Empty the Recycle Bin

1. Right-click the Recycle Bin icon on the Windows Vista desktop and choose Empty Recycle Bin from the menu that appears (see Figure 1-11).

2. In the confirmation dialog box that appears (see Figure 1-12), click Yes. A progress dialog box appears indicating the contents are being deleted. Remember that after you empty the Recycle Bin, all files in it are unavailable to you.

 Up until the moment you permanently delete items by performing the preceding steps, you can retrieve items in the Recycle Bin by right-clicking the desktop icon and choosing Open. Select the item you want to retrieve and then click the Restore This Item link near the top of the Recycle Bin window.

 You can modify the Recycle Bin properties by right-clicking it and choosing Properties. In the dialog box that appears, you can change the maximum size for the Recycle bin, and where it should be stored on your hard drive. You can also deselect the option of having a confirmation dialog box appear when you delete Recycle Bin contents.

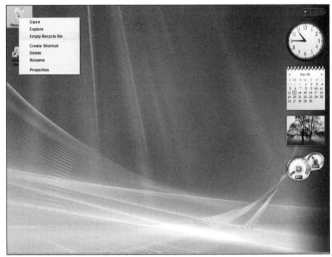

Figure 1-11: The Recycle Bin shortcut menu

Figure 1-12: Confirming the Empty Recycle Bin command.

Shut Down Your Computer

1. Choose Start and then click the arrow to the right of the Lock button.

2. In the resulting shortcut menu shown in Figure 1-13, choose Shut Down to shut the computer down completely; if you want to *reboot* (turn off and turn back on) your computer, choose Restart.

 If you're going away for a while but don't want to have to go through the whole booting up sequence complete with Windows Vista music when you return, you don't have to turn off your computer. Just click the Hibernate button instead (in Step 2) to put your computer into a kind of sleeping state where the screen goes black and the fan shuts down. When you get back, just click your mouse button or press Enter, or in some cases (especially on some laptops) press the Power button; your computer springs to life, and whatever programs and documents you had open are still open.

 If your computer freezes up for some reason, you can turn it off in a couple of ways. Press Ctrl+Alt+Delete twice in a row, or press the power button on your CPU and hold it until the computer shuts down.

 Don't simply turn off your computer at the power source unless you have to because of a computer crash. Windows Vista might not start up properly the next time you turn it on if you don't follow the proper shutdown procedure.

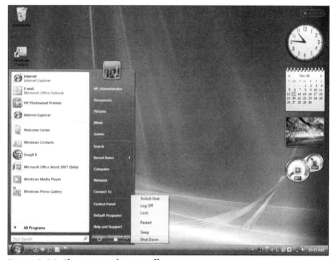

Figure 1-13: The menu used to turn off or restart your computer

Controlling Applications with Windows Vista

*Y*ou might think of Windows Vista as a set of useful accessories, such as games, a calculator, and a paint program for playing around with images, but Windows Vista is first and foremost an operating system. Windows Vista's main purpose is to enable you to run and manage other software applications, from programs that manage your finances to the latest 3-D computer action game. By using the best methods for accessing and running software with Windows Vista, you save time; setting up Windows Vista in the way that works best for you can make your life easier.

In this chapter, you explore several simple and very handy techniques for launching and moving between applications. You go through step-by-step procedures ranging from opening an application to resizing application windows to removing programs when you no longer need them.

This is where you explore all the procedures that you can use to launch, move among, and close down applications in Windows Vista.

Launch an Application

1. Launch an application by using any of the following four methods:

    *   Choose Start⇨All Programs. Locate the program name on the All Programs list that appears and click it. Clicking an item with a folder icon displays a list of programs within it; just click the program on that sublist to open it (as shown in Figure 2-1).

    *   Double-click a program shortcut icon on the desktop (see Figure 2-2).

    *   The taskbar should display by default; if doesn't, press the Windows key (on your keyboard) to display it, and then click an icon on the Quick Launch bar (as shown in Figure 2-2), just to the right of the Start button. Note that the Quick Launch bar is not displayed by default. See the Chapter 1 for more about this.

    *   If you used the program recently and saved a document, choose Recent Items from the Start menu. Then click a document created in that program from the list that displays. (See Chapter 3 for information about displaying recently used files on the Start menu.)

2. When the application opens, if it's a game, play it; if it's a spreadsheet, enter numbers into it; if it's your e-mail program, start deleting junk mail. . . . You get the idea.

Not every program that's installed on your computer appears as a desktop shortcut or Quick Launch bar icon. To add a program to the Quick Launch bar or to add a desktop shortcut, see Chapter 1.

Figure 2-1: The All Programs menu

Figure 2-2: Desktop shortcuts and the taskbar showing the Quick Launch bar

Resize Application Windows

1. With an application open and maximized, click the Restore Down button (the icon showing two overlapping windows) in the top-right corner of the program window. The window reduces in size (see Figure 2-3).

2. To enlarge a window that has been restored down to again fill the screen, click the Maximize button. (*Note:* This button is in the same location as the Restore Down button; this button toggles to one or the other, depending on whether you have the screen reduced in size or maximized. A ScreenTip identifies the button when you pass your mouse over it.)

Switch between Running Applications

1. Open two or more programs. The last program that you open is the active program.

2. Press Alt+Tab to move from one open application window to another.

3. Press and hold Alt+Tab to open a small box, as shown in Figure 2-4, revealing all opened programs.

4. Release the Tab key but keep Alt pressed down. Press Tab to cycle through the icons representing open programs.

5. Release the Alt key, and Windows Vista switches to whichever program is selected. To switch back to the last program that was active, simply press Alt+Tab, and that program becomes the active program once again.

Figure 2-3: A minimized Microsoft Paint window

Figure 2-4: The list of active programs

Move Information between Applications

1. Open two applications. If their windows are maximized, click the Restore Down buttons in the upper-right corners to reduce their sizes.

2. Click any corner on each program window and drag to change the size further until you can see both programs on the Windows desktop at once (see Figure 2-5).

3. Click and hold their title bars to drag the windows around your desktop, or right-click the taskbar and choose Cascade Windows, Show Windows Stacked, or Show Windows Side by Side to automatically arrange the windows on the desktop.

4. Select the information that you want to move (for example text, numbers, or a graphical object) and drag it to the other application document (see Figure 2-6).

5. Release your mouse, and the information is copied to the destination window.

 You can also use simple cut-and-paste or copy-and-paste operations to take information from one application and move it or place a copy of it into a document in another application. In addition, some applications have Export or Send To commands to send the contents of a document to another application. For example, Microsoft Word has a Send To↪Microsoft Office PowerPoint command to quickly send a Word document to be the basis of a PowerPoint presentation outline.

 Remember, this won't work between every type of application. For example, you can't click and drag an open picture in Paint into the Windows Calendar. It will most dependably work when dragging text or objects from one Office 2007 program to another. In other cases, using the cut-and-paste method might be your best bet.

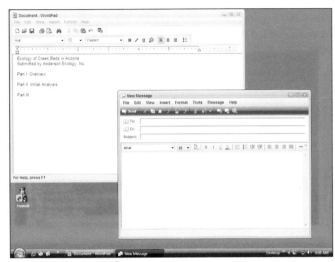

Figure 2-5: Arranging windows

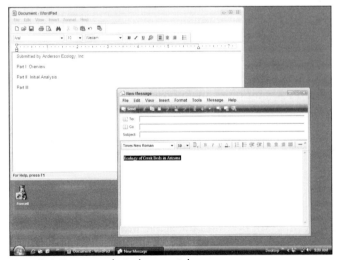

Figure 2-6: Dragging a selection between windows

Start an Application Automatically

1. Using Windows Explorer (right-click Start and then click Explore), locate and open the folder where the application you want to start when you start Windows Vista is located. Click to select it (see Figure 2-7).

2. Drag the item to the Startup folder in the Folders list on the left (under Windows, Start Menu, Programs in the list).

3. Double-click the Startup folder; you see the program listed (see Figure 2-8).

4. When you finish moving programs into the Startup folder, click the Close button in the upper-right corner. The programs you moved will now open every time Windows Vista is started.

 If you place too many programs in Startup, it might take a minute or two before you can get to work because you have to wait for programs to load. Don't overfill your Startup folder: Use it just for the programs you need most often.

 You can remove an application from the Startup folder by right-clicking it and choosing Delete.

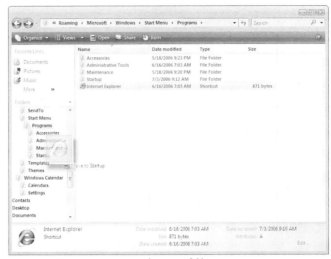

Figure 2-7: Dragging a program to the Startup folder

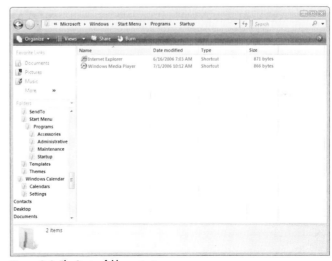

Figure 2-8: The Startup folder contents

Close an Application

1. With an application open, first save any open documents and then close them by using one of these methods:

   - Click the Close button in the upper-right corner of the window.

   - Click Alt+F4 to close most open windows.

   - Choose File⇨Exit (see Figure 2-9).

2. The application closes. If there is a document open that you haven't saved, you see a dialog box asking whether you want to save the document (see Figure 2-10). Click Yes or No, depending on whether you want to save your changes.

 To save a document before closing an application, choose File⇨ Save and use settings in the Save dialog box that appears to name the file and also specify which folder to save it to.

 Note that choosing File⇨Exit closes all open documents in an application. Choose File⇨Close to close only the currently active document and keep the application and any other documents open.

 You don't have to close an application to open or switch to another. To switch between open applications, press Alt+Tab and use the arrow keys to move to the application (or document if multiple documents are open in an application) in which you want to work.

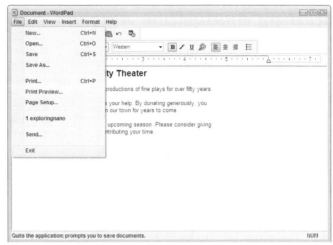

Figure 2-9: Choosing the Exit command

Figure 2-10: Saving changes to open documents

Set Program Defaults

1. Choose Start➪Control Panel➪Programs.

2. In the resulting Programs window, as shown in Figure 2-11, click the Set Your Default Programs link in the Default Programs section to see specifics about the programs that are set as defaults.

3. If a User Account Control window appears, click Continue to allow changes.

4. Select an item in the list of Programs (see Figure 2-12) and click Set This Program as Default.

5. Click OK to save your settings.

 If you want to view what each setting does, or further customize the Custom options, click a program and then click Choose Defaults for This Program to specify file extensions and protocols for the program.

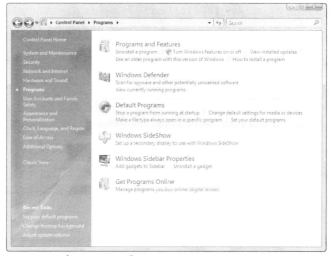

Figure 2-11: The Programs window

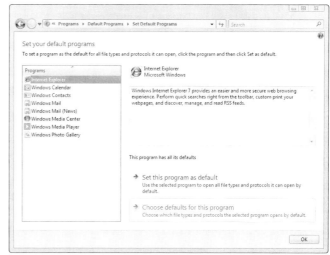

Figure 2-12: The Set Your Default Programs window

Uninstall an Application

1. Choose Start⇨Control Panel⇨Uninstall a Program (under the Programs category).

2. In the resulting window, as shown in Figure 2-13, click a program and then click the Uninstall/Change button. Although some programs will display their own uninstall screen, in most cases, a confirmation dialog box appears (see Figure 2-14).

3. If you're sure that you want to remove the program, click Yes in the confirmation dialog box. A dialog box shows the progress of the procedure; it disappears when the program has been uninstalled.

4. Click the Close button to close the Uninstall or Change a Program window.

 With some programs that include multiple applications, such as Microsoft Office, you might want to remove only one program, not the whole shooting match. For example, you might decide that you have no earthly use for Access but can't let a day go by without using Excel and Word — so why not free up some hard drive space and send Access packing? If you want to modify a program in this way, click the Change button in Step 2 of this task rather than the Uninstall button. The dialog box that appears allows you to select the programs that you want to install or uninstall or might open the original installation screen from your software program.

 Warning: If you click the Change or Remove button, some programs will simply be removed with no further input from you. Be really sure that you don't need a program before you remove it, or that you have the original software on disk/c so you can reinstall it should you need it again.

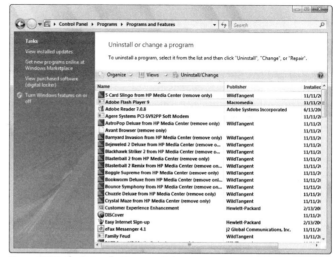

Figure 2-13: The Uninstall a Program window

Figure 2-14: The removal confirmation dialog box

 If you used an earlier version of Windows, you note that the Add a Program command is gone. Because all software created today allows you to put a CD/DVD into your drive and then follow onscreen directions to install the program, Microsoft must have decided that its own Add a Program feature was obsolete!

Working with Files and Folders

*J*oin me for a moment in the office of yesterday. Notice all the metal filing cabinets and manila file folders holding paper rather than the sleek computer workstations and wireless Internet connections we use today.

Fast forward: You still organize the work you do every day in files and folders, but today, the metal and cardboard have been dropped in favor of electronic bits and bytes. *Files* are the individual documents that you save from within applications, such as Word and Excel, and you use folders and subfolders to organize several files into groups or categories, such as by project or by customer.

In this chapter, you find out how to organize and work with files and folders, including

➡ **Finding your way around files and folders:** This includes tasks such as locating and opening files and folders.

➡ **Manipulating files and folders:** These tasks cover moving, renaming, deleting, and printing a file.

➡ **Compressing a file:** This squeezes a file's contents to make larger files more manageable.

Chapter

3

Get ready to . . .

Access Recently Used Items from the Start Menu

1. Open the Start menu and right-click any blank area. From the resulting shortcut menu, choose Properties.

2. In the Taskbar and Start Menu Properties dialog box that appears, click the Start Menu tab (if that tab isn't already displayed).

3. Make sure that the Store and Display a List of Recently Opened Files check box is selected (see Figure 3-1) and then click OK.

4. Choose Start⇨Recent Items, and then choose a file from the resulting submenu (see Figure 3-2) to open it.

 If a file in the Recent Items list can be opened with more than one application — for example, a graphics file that you might open with Paint or in the Windows Picture and Fax Viewer — you can right-click the file and use the Open With command to control which application is used to open the file.

 There's another way to look for documents you've worked with recently. Recently used programs will be listed in the main Start menu. If you open one there will typically be a list of recently used files at the bottom of the application's File or similar menu.

Figure 3-1: The Taskbar and Start Menu Properties dialog box

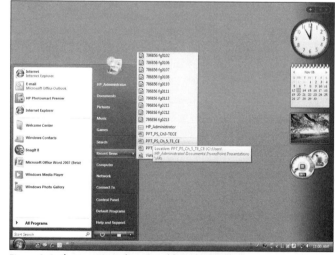

Figure 3-2: The Recent Items list accessed from the Start menu

Locate Files and Folders in Your Computer

1. Choose Start⇨Computer.

2. In the resulting Computer window (see Figure 3-3) double-click an item, such as a floppy drive, a CD-ROM drive, or your computer hard drive, to open it.

3. If the file or folder that you want is stored within another folder (see Figure 3-4 for an example of the resulting window), double-click the folder or a series of folders until you locate it.

4. When you find the file you want, double-click it to open it.

 Note the buttons on the top of the window in Figure 3-4. Use the commands in this area to perform common file and folder tasks, such as organizing, viewing, or opening files; or burning a file to a CD/DVD.

Depending on how you choose to display files and folders, you might see text listings as in Figure 3-4, icons, or even thumbnail representations of file contents.

Figure 3-3: The Computer window

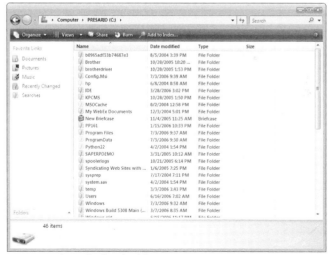

Figure 3-4: The window for a hard drive

Locate Files and Folders in Windows Explorer

1. Right-click the Start menu and choose Explore.

2. In the resulting Windows Explorer window, as shown in Figure 3-5, double-click a folder in the Name field to open the folder.

3. The folder's contents are displayed. If necessary, open a series of folders in this manner until you locate the file you want.

4. When you find the file you want, double-click it to open it.

 To see different perspectives and information about files in Windows Explorer, click the arrow on the Views button (it looks like series of columns) and choose one of the following menu options: Extra Large, Large, Medium, or Small Icons for graphical displays; Details to show details such as Date Modified and Size, and Tiles to show the file/folder name, type, and size. If you are working with a folder containing graphics files, the graphics automatically display as thumbnails unless you choose Details.

 There are some shortcuts to commonly used folders in the Start menu, including Documents, Pictures, and Music. Click one of these and Windows Explorer opens that particular window.

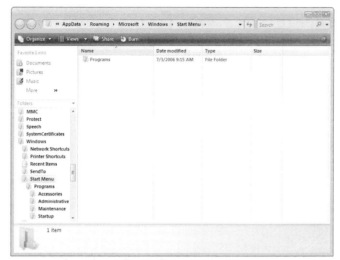

Figure 3-5: The Windows Explorer window

Search for a File

1. Choose Start⇨Search.

2. In the resulting Search Results window, enter a search term in the Search field (see Figure 3-6).

3. Click the arrow for the In field and choose locations to search.

4. Click the type of item for which you want to search along the top of the window (for example Picture, Music, Document, or E-mail). Click the Search Tools button and choose Search Options to modify search parameters. The search begins, and results are displayed (see Figure 3-7).

5. Click any of the column headings (Name, Date Modified, and so on) to sort your results by that item.

6. Click Views to cycle through the options of various size icons or text listings, or click the arrow on this field to choose your preferred view from a list.

7. When you locate the file you want, you can double-click it to open it.

 Search Folders are a new feature in Windows Vista. To save the results of a search, you can click the Save Search button. In the Save As dialog box that appears, provide a filename and type, set the location to save it to, and then click Save. The search results are saved as a search folder on your computer in your user name folder.

 Try using the new feature Instant Search, which provides a search box right on the Start menu. Just click Start, and type a search term in the box labeled Start Search. Click either the Search the Internet or See All Results link that appears. The Search window appears, and you can use the procedures in this task to refine or get results of your search.

Figure 3-6: The Search window

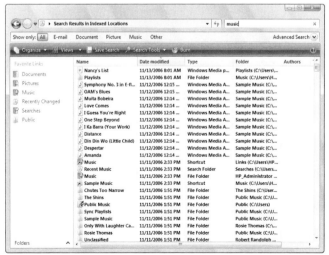

Figure 3-7: The Search Results window

Move a File or Folder

1. Right-click the Start menu button and choose Explore.

2. In the resulting Windows Explorer window (see Figure 3-8), double-click a folder or series of folders to locate the file that you want to move.

3. Take one of the following actions:

   - Click and drag the file to another folder in the Folders pane on the left side of the window. If you right-click and drag, you are offered the options of moving or copying the item when you place it via a shortcut menu that appears.

   - Right-click the file and choose Send To. Then choose from the options shown in the submenu that appears (as shown in Figure 3-9).

4. Click the Close button in the upper-right corner of the Windows Explorer window to close it.

 If you change your mind about moving an item using the right-click-and-drag method, you can click Cancel on the shortcut menu that appears.

 If you want to create a copy of a file or folder in another location on your computer, right-click the item and choose Copy. Use Windows Explorer to navigate to the location where you want to place a copy, right-click and choose Paste or press Ctrl+V.

Figure 3-8: The Windows Explorer window

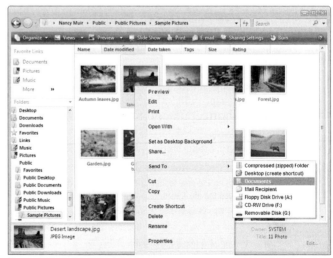

Figure 3-9: The Send To submenu

Rename a File or Folder

1. Locate the file that you want to rename by using Windows Explorer. (Right-click Start and choose Explore.)

2. Right-click the file and choose Rename (see Figure 3-10).

3. The filename is now available for editing. Type a new name, and then click anywhere outside the filename to save the new name.

 You can't rename a file to have the same name as another file located in the same folder. To give a file the same name as another, cut it from its current location, paste it into another folder, and then follow the procedure in this task. Or, open the file and save it to a new location with the same name, which creates a copy. Be careful, though: Two files with the same name can cause confusion when you search for files. If at all possible, use unique filenames.

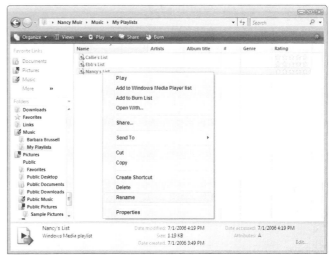

Figure 3-10: A filename available for editing

Create a Shortcut to a File or Folder

1. Locate the file or folder by using Windows Explorer. (Right-click Start and choose Explore.)

2. In the resulting Windows Explorer window (see Figure 3-11), right-click the file or folder that you want to create a shortcut for and then choose Create Shortcut.

3. A shortcut named *File or Folder Name Shortcut* appears at the bottom of the open folder. Click the shortcut and drag it to the desktop.

 To open the file in its originating application or a folder in Windows Explorer, simply double-click the desktop shortcut icon.

 Instead of creating a shortcut and dragging it to the desktop, you can right-click a file or folder and choose Sent To⇨Desktop (Create Shortcut) to accomplish the same thing.

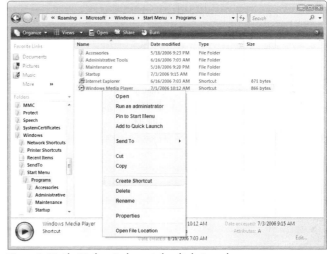

Figure 3-11: The Windows Explorer window displaying a shortcut menu

Print a File

1. Open the file with the application in which it was created.

2. Choose File⇨Print.

3. In the resulting Print dialog box (see Figure 3-12), select what to print; these options might vary but generally include the following

   - **All** prints all pages in the document.

   - **Current Page** prints whatever page your cursor is active in at the moment.

   - **Pages** prints a page range or series of pages you enter in that field. For example, enter 3-11 to print pages 3 through 11; or enter 3, 7, 9-11 to print pages 3, 7, and 9 through 11.

   - **Selection** prints any text or objects that you have selected within the file when you choose the Print command.

4. In the Number of Copies field, click the up or down arrow to set the number of copies to make; if you want multiple copies collated, select the Collate check box.

5. Click OK to proceed with printing.

 Here's another method for printing: locate the file by using Windows Explorer (right-click Start and choose Explore). Right-click the file and choose Print from the shortcut menu that appears. The file prints with your default printer settings.

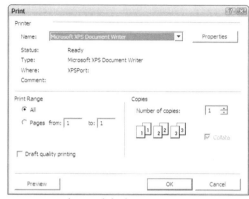

Figure 3-12: The Print dialog box

 Different applications might offer different options in the Print dialog box. For example, PowerPoint offers several options for what to print, including slides, handouts, or the presentation outline, and Outlook allows you to print e-mails in table or in memo style.

Delete a File or Folder

1. Locate the file or folder by using Windows Explorer. (Right-click Start and choose Explore.)

2. In the resulting Windows Explorer window, right-click the file or folder that you want to delete (see Figure 3-13) and then choose Delete.

3. In the resulting dialog box (see Figure 3-14), click Yes to delete the file.

 When you delete a file or folder in Windows Vista, it's not really gone. It's removed to the Recycle Bin. Windows Vista periodically purges older files from this folder, but you might still be able to retrieve recently deleted files and folders from it. To try to restore a deleted file or folder, double-click the Recycle Bin icon on the desktop. Right-click the file or folder and choose Restore. Windows Vista restores the file to wherever it was when you deleted it.

 Instead of right-clicking and choosing Delete from the menu that appears in Step 2 above, you can click the Delete key on your keyboard.

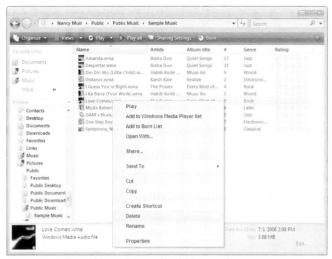

Figure 3-13: The Windows Explorer window displaying a shortcut menu

Figure 3-14: The Delete File dialog box

Create a Compressed File or Folder

1. Locate the files or folders that you want to compress by using Windows Explorer. (Right-click Start and choose Explore.)

2. In the resulting Windows Explorer window, you can do the following (as shown in Figure 3-15):

   • **Select a series of files or folders:** Click a file or folder, press and hold Shift to select a series of items listed consecutively in the folder, and click the final item.

   • **Select nonconsecutive items:** Press the Ctrl key and click each item you want to include.

3. Right-click the selected items. In the resulting shortcut menu (see Figure 3-16), choose Send To⇨Compressed (Zipped) Folder. A new compressed folder appears. The folder icon is named after the last file you selected in the series and the name of the folder is left open for you to edit.

 Following Step 3 in this task, to rename the compressed file just type a new name and then click outside of the file name area. To rename the file at a later time, see the task "Rename a File or Folder," earlier in this chapter.

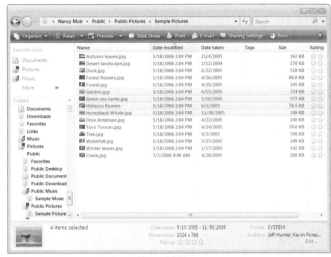

Figure 3-15: A series of selected files and folders

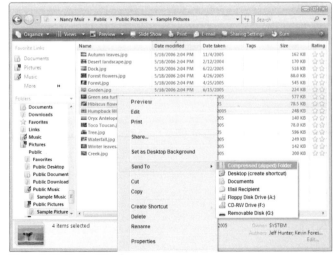

Figure 3-16: The Send To submenu

Add a File to Your Favorites List

1. Locate the files or folders that you want to make a Favorite by using Windows Explorer. (Right-click Start and choose Explore).

2. In the resulting Windows Explorer window, click a file or folder and drag it to the Favorites folder in the Folders list on the left (see Figure 3-17).

3. To see a list of your Favorites, choose Start➪Favorites.

4. In the resulting submenu (see Figure 3-18), click an item to open it.

 If the Favorites item doesn't display on your Start menu, right-click the Start menu and choose Properties. On the Start Menu tab with Start Menu selected, click the Customize button. Make sure that Favorites Menu is selected, and then click OK twice to save the setting.

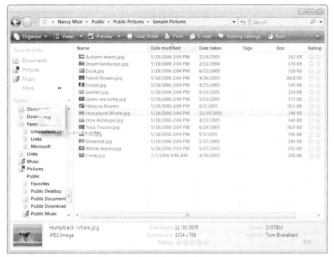

Figure 3-17: The Favorites menu in Windows Explorer

Figure 3-18: The Favorites submenu on the Windows Start menu

Using Built-In Windows Applications

Windows Vista isn't just a traffic cop for your computer's hardware and other software programs; it has its own set of neat tools that you can use to get things done. What sorts of things? Well, by using various Windows Accessories (that is, built-in software programs) you can do everything from writing down great thoughts to working with beautiful pictures. Here's what the Windows built-in applications help you do:

➠ **Work with words.** WordPad provides a virtual pad for jotting down ideas, making notes, creating small documents, or entering programming code. WordPad isn't as robust as some mainstream word processors, but it's just write (pun intended) for simple documents with a few formatting bells and whistles.

➠ **Play with images.** Windows makes you an artist because you can view and edit graphics files in Paint and view digital images (you know, the photos you took at little Ricky's birthday party?) in the Windows Photo Gallery. The new Snipping Tool is a way to grab little clippings of either words or images, annotate them, and then add them to a variety of documents.

➠ **Manage contacts and your schedule.** Windows Contacts is an electronic version of that little alphabetical book you keep by your phone; it's a great place to store contact information. Windows Calendar provides an easy-to-use scheduling tool in which you can enter tasks and share task information with others.

Get ready to . . .

Create a Formatted Document in WordPad

1. Choose Start⇨All Programs⇨Accessories⇨WordPad to open the WordPad window, as shown in Figure 4-1.

2. Enter text in the blank document. (*Note:* Press Enter to create blank lines between paragraphs.)

3. Click and drag to select the text; then choose Format⇨ Font.

4. In the resulting Font dialog box, as shown in Figure 4-2, adjust the settings for Font, Font Style, or Size. You can apply strikeout or underline effects by selecting those check boxes. You can also modify the font color and even apply a script from a language that uses an alphabet different than English, such as Arabic. Click OK to apply the settings.

5. Click various other tools, such as the alignment buttons or the Bullets button on the toolbar, to format selected text.

6. Choose Insert⇨Object to insert an object.

7. In the Object dialog box that appears, select the Create New option, click an object type, and then click OK. Modify the inserted object however you want (moving it, resizing it, and so on).

8. When your document is complete, choose File⇨Save. In the Save As dialog box, enter a name in the File Name text box, select a file location from the Address Bar drop-down list, and then click Save.

 E-mailing a copy of your WordPad document is simplicity itself. Just choose File⇨Send, and an e-mail form appears from your default e-mail program with the file already attached. Just enter a recipient and a message and click Send. It's on its way!

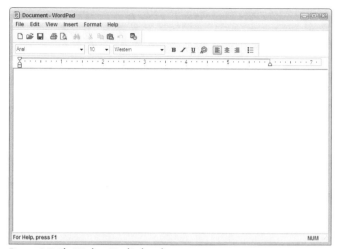

Figure 4-1: The Windows WordPad window

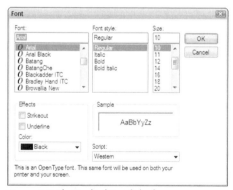

Figure 4-2: The WordPad Font dialog box

Edit a Picture in Paint

1. Choose Start⇨All Programs⇨Accessories⇨Paint.

2. In the resulting Paint window, choose File⇨Open. Locate a picture file that you want to edit (see Figure 4-3), select it, and click Open. There's a pretty picture of my cat shown in the Paint window in Figure 4-4.

     You can also get an image from a camera or scanner by using the File⇨From Scanner or Camera command.

3. Now you can edit the picture in any number of ways:

    *   **Edit colors.** Choose a color from the color palette at the top of the Paint window and use various tools (such as Airbrush, Brush, Fill with Color, and the Pick Color dropper) to apply color to the image or selected drawn objects, such as rectangles. Clicking on a color selects a foreground color; right-clicking a color selects a background color.

    *   **Select areas.** Select the Free-Form Select and Select tools, and then click and drag on the image to select portions of the picture. You can then crop out these elements by choosing Edit⇨Cut.

    *   **Add text.** Select the Text tool, and then click and drag the image to create a text box in which you can enter and format text.

    *   **Draw objects.** Select the Rectangle, Rounded Rectangle, Polygon, or Ellipse tool, and then click and drag the image to draw objects.

    *   **Modify the image.** Use the commands on the Image menu to change the colors and stretch out, flip around, or change the size of the image.

4. Choose File⇨Save to save your masterpiece, File⇨Print to print it, or File⇨Send to send it by e-mail.

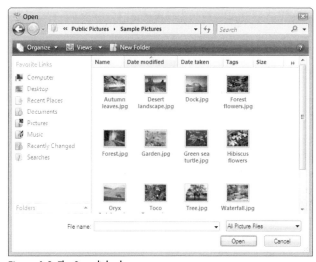

Figure 4-3: The Open dialog box

Figure 4-4: A picture opened in Paint

View a Digital Image in the Windows Photo Gallery

1. Choose Start➪All Programs➪Windows Photo Gallery.

2. In the resulting Windows Photo Gallery window, as shown in Figure 4-5, you can use the tools at the bottom (see Figure 4-6) to do any of the following:

   • The Next and Previous icons move to a previous or following image in the same folder.

   • The Display Size icon in the shape of a magnifying glass displays a slider you can click and drag to change the size of the image thumbnails.

   • The Delete button deletes the selected image.

   • The Rotate Clockwise and Rotate Counterclockwise icons spin the image 90 degrees at a time.

   • The center Play Slide Show button with a slide image on it displays the images in your Picture folder in a continuous slide show.

3. Click any of the items on the left to choose which images to display (such as those taken in a certain year or saved in a certain folder).

 Did you upload a photo from your camera but you don't remember what you called it? If you want to find a photo you imported to the Photo Gallery from a camera or scanner in the recent past, click the Recently Imported folder in the picture list on the left.

Figure 4-5: The Windows Photo Gallery

Figure 4-6: The tools you can use to manipulate images

 For more on the Windows Photo Gallery, see Chapter 22.

4. Some of the buttons at the top of the window (see Figure 4-7) are listed here; see Chapter 22 for a description of all the menus and features of Windows Photo Gallery.

- **File** displays commands for working with the file, such as Delete and Rename.

- **Fix** displays the selected image with image manipulation tools.

- **Info** displays information about the image, such as the date created and size.

- **Print** is the button to click to print the selected image.

- **Create** allows you to create a DVD, movie, or data disc using the image.

- **E-mail** opens a dialog box to specify the image to be attached to an e-mail using your default mail program.

- **Open** allows you to open the image in another program, such as Paint, which you can use to edit the image.

5. When you finish viewing and working with images, click the Close button in the top right corner to close the Photo Gallery (see Figure 4-8).

 If you make a change to a photo in the gallery using the Fix feature, Windows saves a copy of the original photo in case you want to restore it. By default the original photo is never ever deleted, but you can change that to save space. Choose File⇨Option, and in the Windows Photo Gallery Options dialog box, select a different setting in the Move Originals to Recycle Bin After drop-down list, such as one month or six months.

Figure 4-7: Use these buttons and drop down menus to work with your photos in a variety of ways.

Figure 4-8: Close the Windows Photo Gallery

Enter Contacts in Windows Contacts

1. Choose Start⇨All Programs⇨Windows Contacts.

2. In the resulting Windows Contacts window, as shown in Figure 4-9, right-click and choose New⇨Contact.

3. In the Properties dialog box shown in Figure 4-10, enter information in various fields, clicking other various tabs to add more details. For some fields, such as E-mail, you must enter information and then click the Add button to add it to a list.

4. After you finish entering information, click OK.

 The IDs tab of the Contacts Properties dialog box allows you to associate digital IDs with e-mail addresses. A digital ID proves your identity to recipients of your e-mail, and you can use them to encrypt your message as well

Figure 4-9: Windows Contacts

Figure 4-10: Entering new contact information

Clip with the Windows Snipping Tool

1. Choose Start⇨All Programs⇨Accessories⇨Snipping Tool.

2. In the Snipping Tool window that appears (see Figure 4-11), click the down-arrow on the New button and choose a snip mode from the drop-down list:

- **Free Form Snip** lets you draw any old kind of line you like, such as a triangle, to define what you want to snip.

- **Rectangular Snip** does what it says: When you click and drag over a region, it forms a rectangular snip.

- **Window Snip** allows you to select an active window to snip.

- **Full-Screen Snip** takes the entire enchilada, capturing the whole screen in the wink of an eye.

3. If you chose Free Form or Rectangular in Step 2, click and drag on the desktop or in a document to form an area to snip. If you chose Windows, click on the window you want to snip. If you chose Full-Screen, the snip happens automatically.

4. In the mark-up window that appears (see Figure 4-12), use the Pen, Highlighter, and Eraser tools to mark up the image.

5. Click the Save Snip button that looks like a computer disk to display the Save As dialog box, where you can enter a filename, specify the location to save the file to, and then click Save.

Figure 4-11: The Snipping Tool window

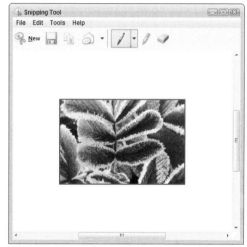

Figure 4-12: The mark-up window with a captured snip

Track Your Time in Windows Calendar

1. Choose Start➪All Programs➪Windows Calendar.

2. In the Windows Calendar window shown in Figure 4-13, click the New Task or the New Appointment button.

3. In the Details pane shown in Figure 4-14, enter information about the task or appointment, including whether Windows Calendar should remind you about the item.

4. Click anywhere outside of the New Task/New Appointment pane. The item appears in your daily calendar.

5. Click the View button to cycle through the views, or click the down-arrow on the View button to choose a view, such as Month or Week.

 If you want to share your calendar, you can choose Share➪Publish and enter a URL for the location where you want to publish your calendar online. You can even make a setting so that any changes to the calendar are automatically published online.

 You can import a calendar you create in another program, such as Outlook by choosing File➪Import. In the resulting Import dialog box, enter the name of the file, and choose whether to create a new calendar, or integrate the calendar entries into another calendar.

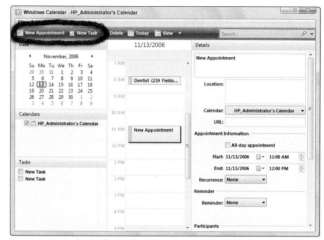

Figure 4-13: The Windows Calendar window

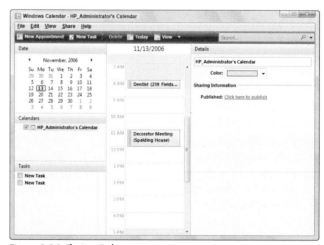

Figure 4-14: The New Task pane

Using the Windows Sidebar and Gadgets

Windows Vista has a new desktop feature called the *Windows Sidebar*. The Sidebar contains tools, called *gadgets*, displayed as icons along the right side of your screen by default (although you can make settings to display it on the left). From the Windows Sidebar, you can quickly access various handy features to write down great thoughts, calculate numbers, feed online data direct to your desktop, and more. Here's what you can do with the Windows gadgets:

- **Work with words and images.** Notes is like an onscreen sticky notepad, where you can jot reminders or ideas on the fly. Slide Show is a continuous slide show of the photos in your Pictures folder.

- **Manipulate numbers.** The Windows Calculator doesn't fit in the palm of your hand, but it does offer a little onscreen calculator that you can use to push numbers around. Punch numbers in by using your mouse or keyboard instead of your finger, and you can handle even complex calculations with ease.

- **Play with puzzles.** Two neat little puzzles, Number Puzzle and Picture Puzzle, allow you to play games that are so tiny, even your boss won't notice you're not actually working.

- **Work with online data.** The Feed Watcher and Feed Viewer allow you to grab data from online RSS feeds (a format used for syndication of news and other content), such as the latest news or other useful information. Stocks and Currency Conversion provide up-to-the-minute data on stocks and currency values.

- **Plus one more gadget.** The CPU Meter provides up-to-date information about your computer processor speed and available memory.

Get ready to . . .

Set Up the Windows Sidebar

1. Right-click the Windows Sidebar icon on the Windows taskbar and choose Properties to open the Windows Sidebar Properties dialog box shown in Figure 5-1.

2. Select the Sidebar Is Always on Top of Other Windows check box. If you like, you can also enable Start Sidebar When Windows Starts to ensure that the Sidebar always displays when you start your computer.

3. Click OK and then click the Close button to close the Control Panel window. The Sidebar appears, as shown in Figure 5-2.

 If you're left handed, or have some other propensity for things on the left, you can choose to have the Sidebar displayed on the left side of the screen by selecting the Left radio button in the Windows Sidebar Properties dialog box.

 Once you've made your sidebar settings, the quickest way to display the Sidebar in the future is to click the Windows Sidebar icon on the Windows taskbar

Figure 5-1: Setting up Sidebar to appear on your desktop

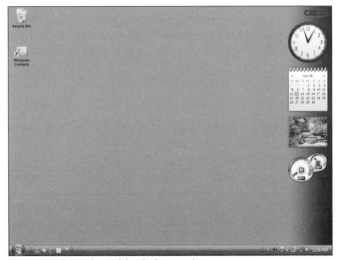

Figure 5-2: The Windows Sidebar displaying gadgets

Add Gadgets to the Sidebar

1. With the Sidebar displayed, click the Gadgets symbol (a plus sign) at the top of the Sidebar.

2. In the resulting Add Gadgets dialog box (see Figure 5-3), double-click a gadget (or click and drag it to the Sidebar). If you want to view additional gadgets, click the arrows on the Page # of # item in the top left corner of the dialog box.

3. Click the Close button to close the dialog box.

Figure 5-3: The Add Gadgets dialog box

 Gadgets included in Windows Vista may change; if any gadgets discussed in this chapter don't appear, click the Get More Gadgets Online link to find and install them.

 You can detach gadgets from the Sidebar and place them on the desktop. If you then close the Sidebar, you can still work with those desktop gadgets. To move a gadget, just click the Move button (the bottom of the three buttons to the right of any gadget) and drag the gadget where you want it.

 If you add more gadgets than can be shown in the single Sidebar, use the Previous and Next arrows at the top of the Sidebar to move from one set of gadgets to the next.

Make a Note with Notes

1. Add the Notes gadget to the Sidebar (see the preceding task) and click it.

2. Type whatever note you wish (see Figure 5-4), and then do any of the following:

   • **Save:** Click the Add button (the plus symbol on the note) to save the note and move on to the next blank note.

   • **Navigate:** Click the Back arrow to move back to the first note — or when you've entered more than one note, click the Forward arrow to move to the next note.

   • **Delete:** Click the Delete button to delete a note.

3. To change the font or color of your Notes text, click the Settings button (the little wrench in the set of tools to the right of any gadget).

4. In the resulting Notes window (see Figure 5-5), use the Font and Font Size fields to modify the font. Click the arrows beneath the Notes preview to choose a different Notes background. Click OK when you're done.

5. Click OK to save the settings.

 You can right-click the Notes gadget and use a shortcut menu to undo, cut, copy, paste, delete, or select all the displayed note text. You can also use shortcut key combinations for many of these, such as Ctrl+X for Cut.

 If you want two or more sets of Notes for different topics or types of notes, just add Notes to the Sidebar a second time (see the preceding task). Each set of Notes added can be a different color, so you can easily keep track of which Notes pad holds which type of information.

Figure 5-4: Text entered on Notes

Figure 5-5: The Notes dialog box

Display a Continuous Slide Show

Figure 5-6: The Slide Show toolbar

1. Add the Slide Show gadget to the Sidebar (see the earlier task, "Add Gadgets to the Sidebar") and click it.

2. Use the tools along the bottom of the slide show (see Figure 5-6) to do the following:

   - Click the **View button** to display the current slide in the Photo Gallery Viewer.

   - Click **Pause** to stop the slide show at the current slide.

   - Click **Previous** to go to the previous slide.

   - Click **Next** to go to the next slide.

3. Click the Settings button. In the resulting Slide Show dialog box (see Figure 5-7), change the picture folders to include in the slide show, or modify the number of seconds to display each slide or a transition effect to use between slides.

4. Click OK to close the dialog box.

Figure 5-7: The Slide Show dialog box

When you click the View button to display the current slide in Photo Gallery Viewer, you can use tools to modify the image, print it, e-mail it, or even create a movie. See Chapter 22 for more about using Photo Gallery Viewer.

Use the Windows Calculator

Figure 5-8: The Calculator gadget

1. Add the Calculator gadget (see Figure 5-8) to the Sidebar. (See the earlier task, "Add Gadgets to the Sidebar.") You can enter numbers and symbols in a few different ways.

    *   **Type numbers and symbols on your keyboard.** They appear in the entry box of the calculator. Press Enter to perform the calculation.

    *   **Click numbers or symbols on the calculator display and then click the = button to perform the calculation.** You can also use your keyboard to enter numbers and operands.

You can right-click gadgets and choose the Detach from Sidebar command from the shortcut menu to move a gadget to the desktop, rather than using the click-and-drag method. This shortcut menu also allows you to modify the opacity of a gadget so that when you move your mouse off it, it fades to the degree that you set the opacity.

Play with Puzzles

1. Add the Picture Puzzle gadget to the Sidebar. (See the earlier task, "Add Gadgets to the Sidebar.")

2. Click either of the tools along the top of the puzzle (see Figure 5-9) to do the following:

   • **Show Picture** displays the picture you're trying to create.

   • **Solve** rearranges the pieces into the picture. After you have clicked Solve, you can click this button again (it's then labelled Shuffle) to rearrange the pieces.

3. To play the game, click any piece adjacent to a blank square. It moves into the blank space. Keep clicking and moving pieces until you get the picture pieces arranged to form a picture.

4. Click the Settings button to the right of the puzzle to display its settings dialog box (see Figure 5-10).

5. Click the Previous or Next button to scroll through available pictures for the puzzle.

6. When you find the picture you want, click OK to close the dialog box.

Figure 5-9: The Picture Puzzle gadget

Figure 5-10: The Picture Puzzle dialog box.

Convert Currency

1. Add the Currency Conversion gadget to the Sidebar. (See the earlier task, "Add Gadgets to the Sidebar.")

2. Connect to the Internet to access the latest currency rates (as shown in Figure 5-11) and do any of the following.

   • Enter the number of dollars; the number of equivalent euros is displayed.

   • Click the arrow to the right of either currency and choose another currency to convert from or to (see Figure 5-12).

 To view the online source for the latest currency conversion rates, click and drag the Currency gadget to the desktop and click the Data Providers link. The MSN Money page opens. Click the Banking tab and then click the Currency Exchange Rates link to view current rates.

 If you detach the Currency Converter from the Sidebar an Add tool appears. Click this to select another currency to display. With this feature you can compare multiple currencies at the same time.

Figure 5-11: The Currency Conversion gadget connected to the Internet

Figure 5-12: Choosing a different currency to convert.

Add a Feed to the Windows Sidebar

1. Add the Feed Headlines gadget to the Sidebar and click View Headlines. (See the earlier task, "Add Gadgets to the Sidebar.")

2. Double-click a feed to display it in your browser (see Figure 5-13).

3. At the Web site that appears you can view blog entries, submit an entry, or subscribe to additional feeds.

4. Click the Settings button. In the resulting Feed Viewer dialog box (see Figure 5-14), select the default feed and the number of recent headlines to show.

5. Click OK to close the dialog box.

Use the Next and Previous arrows that appear at the bottom of the Feed Headlines gadget when you move your mouse over it to scroll through available feeds.

For more information about RSS feeds, click the What are Feeds? link in the Feed Headlines settings dialog box.

Figure 5-13: The Feed Viewer showing the IEBlog

Figure 5-14: The Feed Viewer dialog box

Get the Latest Stock Quotes

1. Add the Stocks gadget to the Sidebar. (See the earlier task, "Add Gadgets to the Sidebar.") Click and drag it to the desktop where you can view more information.

2. Connect to the Internet; stock prices and stock exchange data are displayed (see Figure 5-15).

3. Click the Search for a Stock button (a plus sign in the bottom-right corner) and enter a stock symbol. Click the Search button and the price is displayed (as shown in Figure 5-16).

4. Click on a stock exchange to display detailed information about it in your browser.

5. Click the Close button to close your browser.

 Click the Show Stock Graph icon (a squiggly line symbol in the bottom-right corner of the Stocks gadget) to view a graph of activity for the day.

Figure 5-15: The Stock gadget on the desktop displaying stocks

Figure 5-16: The Stocks dialog box

Monitor Your CPU

1. Add the CPU Meter gadget (see Figure 5-17) to the Sidebar. (See the earlier task, "Add Gadgets to the Sidebar.")

2. Use the readouts to monitor the following:

   • CPU Usage monitors how hard your CPU is working to process various programs and processes running on your computer.

   • Random Access Memory (RAM) monitors the percent of your computer memory that is being used.

 That's about all there is to CPU Meter! You can't make any settings for it. It's just a little reminder that helps you keep track of your computer's performance. If memory is almost at 100%, consider freeing some space. If the CPU is at a higher percentage, odds are you've got lots of programs running which could be slowing down your computer's performance; consider shutting some down!

Figure 5-17: The CPU Meter gadget

 If you want more detail about your computer memory usage, use the Start menu to display the Control Panel and choose System and Maintenance. The System links allow you to monitor the processor speed and the amount of RAM available.

Part II
Getting on the Internet

The 5th Wave   By Rich Tennant

"My spam filter checks the recipient address, http links, and any writing that panders to postmodern English romanticism with conceits to 20th century graphic narrative."

Accessing the Internet

Chapter 6

The Internet has become as integral to computing as a cellphone is to a teenager. It's how people communicate, transfer files, share images and music, shop for goods and services, and research everything from aardvarks to zebras.

Getting connected to the Internet isn't hard. Most Internet service providers (ISPs) provide software to set up your connection automatically. But you can connect in a few different ways, and you'll encounter a few different technologies. You might also need to tinker around with some settings to get things working just the way you want them to.

In this chapter, you find out how to make and manage Internet connections, including

- ➡ **Setting up your connection:** The New Connection Wizard helps you with this process. Then you can designate your default connection so that you log on to the Internet using the method that you prefer.

- ➡ **Modifying settings:** Whether you use a TCP/IP or an always-on connection (such as cable or DSL), you discover the ins and outs of configuring them here as well as how to share your Internet connection with someone else.

- ➡ **Using your Internet connection to connect to a network:** If you're like many people, you might need to tap into your workplace network from a remote location. It's easy to do, and I tell you how.

Get ready to . . .

Set Up a New ISP Internet Connection

1. Choose Start⇨Network.

2. In the resulting window, click Network and Sharing Center.

3. In the resulting Network and Sharing Center window (see Figure 6-1), click the Set Up a Connection or Network link.

4. In the Choose a Connection Option dialog box, accept the default option Connect to the Internet by clicking Next.

5. In the resulting dialog box, click your connection. (These steps follow the selection of Broadband.) If you have a current connection, a window appears asking whether you want to use a current connection. Click Next to accept the default option of creating a new connection.

6. In the resulting dialog box, as shown in Figure 6-2, enter your user name, password, and connection name (if you want to assign one) and then click Connect. Windows Vista automatically detects the connection, and the Network and Sharing Center appears with your connection listed.

 In many cases, if you have a disc from your ISP, you don't need to follow the preceding steps. Just pop that CD into your CD-ROM drive, and in no time, a window appears that gives you instructions for setting up your account.

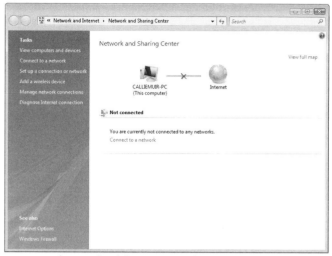

Figure 6-1: The Network and Sharing Center window

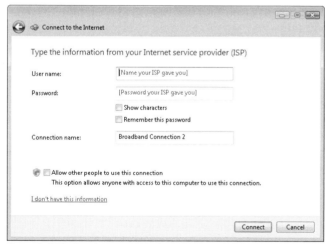

Figure 6-2: The New Connection Wizard

Share an Internet Connection on a Network

1. Choose Start⇨Network.

2. In the resulting window, click the Network and Sharing Center link.

3. In the resulting Network Connections window (refer to Figure 6-1), click the Manage Network Connections link.

4. In the resulting window (see Figure 6-3), right-click a connection and then choose Properties.

5. In the Connection Properties dialog box, click the Sharing tab (see Figure 6-4).

6. Select the Allow Other Network Users to Connect through This Computer's Internet Connection check box.

7. If you want to dial this connection automatically when another computer on your network tries to access it, select the Establish a Dial-up Connection Whenever a Computer on My Network Attempts to Access the Internet check box.

8. If you want other people on your network to control the shared Internet connection by enabling or disabling it, select the Allow Other Network Users to Control or Disable the Shared Internet Connection check box.

9. Click OK, and then close the Network Connections window to save the shared connection settings.

 Users on your network also have to make some settings to use your shared connection. They have to configure settings for an Internet communications standard called TCP/IP (Transmission Control Protocol/Internet Protocol) on their local area connections so that they get an IP connection automatically.

Figure 6-3: The Network Connections window

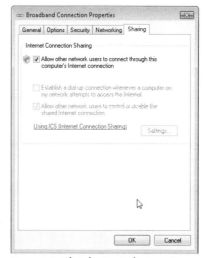

Figure 6-4: Selected options in the Connection Properties dialog box

Configure a TCP/IP Connection

1. Choose Start⇨Network.

2. In the resulting window, click the Network and Sharing Center link.

3. In the resulting Network and Sharing Center window (refer to Figure 6-1), click the Manage Network Connections link.

4. In the resulting window, right-click a connection and then choose Properties.

5. In the Connection Properties dialog box, click the Networking tab (see Figure 6-5).

6. On the Networking tab, in the This Connection Uses the Following Items area, select the Internet Protocol Version (TCP/IP) option and then click the Properties button. Be sure that the latest version of the TCP/IP is selected, even if earlier versions are also available and selected.

7. In the Internet Protocol (TCP/IP) Properties dialog box that appears (as shown in Figure 6-6), allow addresses to be assigned automatically. Select the Obtain an IP Address Automatically option and then click OK twice.

 Although you can enter addresses manually in the Internet Protocol (TCP/IP) Properties dialog box, I recommend letting them be assigned automatically. That way, if your setup changes, you don't have to go back and manually modify addresses. This also saves you the hassle of having to manually configure certain settings, such as the Domain Name Service, which implements the Domain Name System (DNS). Don't want to worry about such techie things? Me, neither. That's why I just let addresses be assigned automatically.

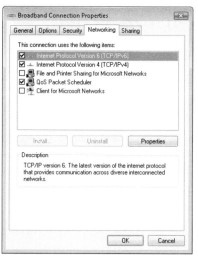

Figure 6-5: The Connection Properties dialog box, Networking tab

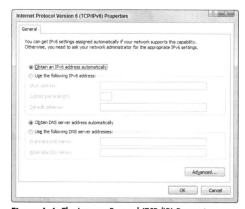

Figure 6-6: The Internet Protocol (TCP/IP) Properties dialog box

Set Up an Always-On Connection

1. Choose Start⇨Network.

2. In the resulting window, click the Network and Sharing Center link.

3. In the resulting window, click Set Up a Connection or Network.

4. In the resulting dialog box, as shown in Figure 6-7, click Next to set up a connection to the Internet. If you have any existing connections at this point, you might be asked whether you want to choose an existing connection or set up a new one. Click Next to set up a new one.

5. In the resulting dialog box (see Figure 6-8), select the Broadband option. In the resulting dialog box, enter your user and password information and a connection name if you wish, and then click Connect.

6. In the following dialog boxes, the wizard notifies you that Windows Vista will detect your connection and make settings for you. When you reach the final wizard dialog box, click Finish to complete the process.

 You might not have to do any of the preceding steps to set up an always-on connection. If your provider doesn't require a user name and password to be entered, simply connect your broadband or cable modem and then restart your computer. Windows Vista should automatically detect the connection.

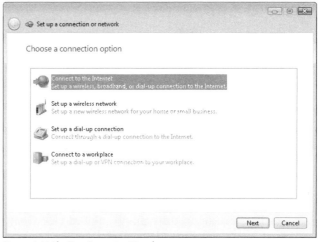

Figure 6-7: The New Connection Wizard

Figure 6-8: Choosing your connection.

Repair a Connection

1. Choose Start⇨Network.

2. In the resulting window, click the Network and Sharing Center link.

3. In the resulting window, click the Manage Network Connections link.

4. In the Network Connections window, right-click the connection and then click the Diagnose button.

5. A diagnostic runs and displays a window with suggestions about how to repair your connection (see Figure 6-9). Click a suggestion to perform the action, and then click the Close button to close the dialog box (for example, resetting the network adapter). If the suggestion is an action you must perform, such as plugging in a cable, do so.

 Sometimes diagnosing a connection doesn't do the trick. In that case, it's best to delete the connection and just create it again by clicking the Create a New Connection link in the Network Connections window and entering the correct settings.

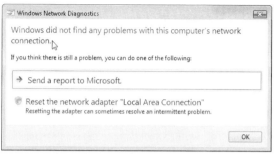

Figure 6-9: The Windows Network Diagnostics window

 You may have recently made or changed a setting that caused your network connection to fail. If that could be the case, you might consider running a System Restore to an earlier point in time. A System Restore will take you back to a time before you changed your settings, but it doesn't delete any programs or documents. See Chapter 18 for more about using the System Restore feature.

Set Up a Connection to the Network at Your Workplace

1. Choose Start➪Network.

2. In the resulting window, click the Network and Sharing Center button.

3. In the resulting window, click Set Up a Connection or Network link. In the Choose a Connection Option window that appears, click Connect to a Workplace and then click Next.

4. In the How Do You Want to Connect? dialog box, as shown in Figure 6-10, click Use My Internet Connection (VPN) (assuming you are connecting over the Internet and not through a phone line).

5. In the next dialog box, enter an address for the connection (see Figure 6-11), and then complete one of two tasks:

   • For a dial-up connection, enter a phone number (see Figure 6-11).

   • For a VPN connection, select whether to automatically dial the initial connection.

6. When you reach the final wizard dialog box, click Finish to complete the wizard.

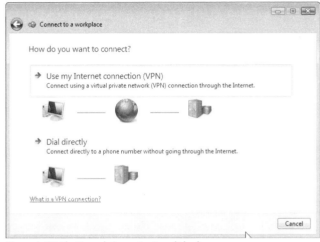

Figure 6-10: The Network Connection Type dialog box

Figure 6-11: The Type the Telephone Number to Connect To dialog box

Designate Your Default Connection

1. Choose Start⇨Network.

2. In the resulting window, click the Network and Sharing Center link.

3. In the resulting window (see Figure 6-12), click the Manage Network Connections link.

4. In the Network Connections window (see Figure 6-13), right-click the connection you want as default and then choose Set as Default Connection. The number (1) appears in parentheses by the connection name.

 Your computer uses the default connection anytime you click a link to an online location or open your browser. However, you can still manually open any connection by opening the Network Connections window, right-clicking any connection, and choosing Connect.

 Why would you need to change a connection? If you travel with a laptop computer you may want to change your default connection from your home network to a wireless connection provided at an airport or hotel, for example. Or, you may use one connection at home and one at the office.

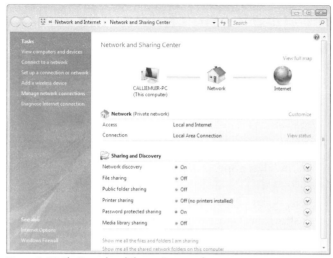

Figure 6-12: The Network and Sharing Center window

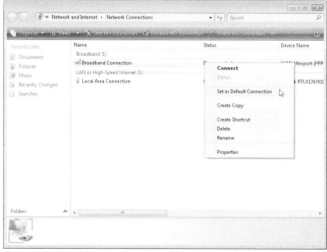

Figure 6-13: The Network Connections window

Remove an Internet Connection

1. Choose Start⊅Network.

2. In the resulting window, click the Network and Sharing Center link.

3. In the resulting window (see Figure 6-14), click the Manage Network Connections link.

4. In the Network Connections window (see Figure 6-15), right-click the connection and then click Delete. The connection name is removed from the Network Connections list.

 Even if you no longer need a connection, as long as you don't click on it, there's no harm leaving it in your connections list. However, somebody else using your computer may be unsure as to which connection to activate, and your Network Connections window will be more cluttered if you don't get rid of old connections.

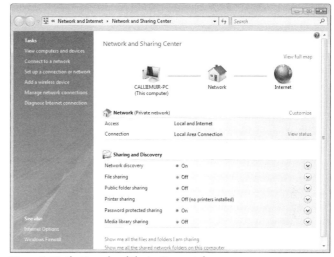

Figure 6-14: The Network and Sharing Center window

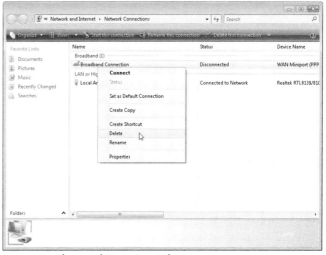

Figure 6-15: The Network Connections window

Browsing the Web with Internet Explorer

*T*o drive around the Internet superhighway, you need a good vehicle. A *browser* is a program that you can use to get around the Internet, and Internet Explorer (IE) is one of the best.

IE is built into Windows Vista because it's made by Microsoft, so the Microsoft folks can put it anywhere they like. This is good news for you because by using IE you can

➠ **Navigate all around the Web.** Use the IE navigation features to jump from one site to another, go back to places you've been (via the Favorites and History features), and search for new places to visit.

➠ **Download files to your computer or print.** When you find what you want online, such as a graphic image or free software program, you might want to save it to your computer for future use. Do you need a hard copy of what you've found? Just use the Print feature of IE.

➠ **Protect yourself.** The Internet is a bit dangerous — a place where some people try to get at your private information and make nefarious use of it. IE provides privacy settings and special features to control the use of *cookies* (small files that folks who run Web sites insert on your hard drive to help them track your online activities). You can use the Content Advisor to limit the online locations that your computer can visit.

Get ready to . . .

Navigate the Web

1. Open IE by clicking the Internet Explorer icon on the Quick Launch portion of the Windows Vista taskbar.

2. Enter a Web site address in the Address bar as shown in Figure 7-1 (www.pubstudio.com is my company's Web site) and then press Enter.

3. On the resulting Web site, click a link, display another page on the site, or enter another address to proceed to another page.

    A link can be an icon or text. A text link is identifiable by colored text, usually blue or purple. After you click a link, it usually changes color to show that it's been followed.

4. Click the Back button to move back to the first page that you visited. Click the Forward button to go forward to the second page that you visited.

5. Click the down-pointing arrow at the far right of the Address bar to display a list of sites that you visited recently, as shown in Figure 7-2. Click a site in this list to go there.

    The Refresh and Stop buttons on the right end of the Address bar are useful for navigating sites. Clicking the Refresh button redisplays the current page. This is especially useful if a page updates information frequently, such as on a stock market site. You can also use the Refresh button if a page doesn't load correctly; it might load correctly when refreshed. Clicking the Stop button stops a page that's loading. So, if you made a mistake entering the address, or if the page is taking longer than you'd like to load, click the Stop button to halt the process.

    You can use the Pop-Up Blocker to stop annoying pop-up ads as you browse. Click the Tools menu button and choose Pop-up Blocker⇨ Turn On Pop-up Blocker to activate this feature. You can also use the Pop-up Blocker Settings command on this same menu to specify sites on which you want to allow pop-ups.

Figure 7-1: My Web site home page

Figure 7-2: Recently visited sites

Search the Web

1. Open IE and click in the Live Search pane on the toolbar.

2. Enter a search term in the text box and then click Search.

3. In the resulting Windows Live list of links (see Figure 7-3), click a link to go that Web page. If you don't see the link that you need, click and drag the scrollbar to view more results.

4. Click a tab along the top of the search results to see different types of results: for example, news stories or images related to your search term.

5. Click the Options link at the top of the Search window to change Live Search settings.

6. In the resulting Search Settings dialog box, as shown in Figure 7-4, select options such as the following, and then click Save to apply the new settings:

   • **SafeSearch:** These options let you set filtering of search results at three levels: Strict, which filters out most inappropriate content; Moderate, which filters out only certain types of content; and Off, which turns off filtering for searches.

   • **Results:** Select one of these options to determine whether results are opened in the current browser window or whether Windows Live opens a new browser window.

 Knowing how search engines work can save you time. For example, if you search by entering *golden retriever*, you typically get sites that contain both words or either word. If you put a plus sign between these two keywords (*golden+retriever*), you get only sites that contain both words.

Figure 7-3: Search results displayed in Windows Live

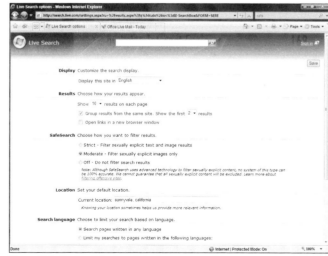

Figure 7-4: The Search Settings dialog box

Find Content on a Web Page

1. With IE open and the Web page that you want to search displayed, click the arrow on the Search box and choose Find on This Page.

2. In the resulting Find dialog box, as shown in Figure 7-5, enter the word that you want to search for. Use the following options to narrow your results:

   - **Match Whole Word Only:** Select this option if you want to find only the whole word (for example, if you enter **elect** and want to find only *elect* and not *electron* or *electronics*).

   - **Match Case:** Select this option if you want to match the case (for example, if you enter **Catholic** and want to find only the always-capitalized religion and not the adjective *catholic*).

3. Click the Next button. The first instance of the word is highlighted on the page (see Figure 7-6). If you want to find another instance, click the Next button again. Click the Previous button to move back to the last match.

4. When you're done searching, click the Close button in the Find dialog box.

Many Web sites, such as www.Amazon.com, have a Search This Site feature that allows you to search not only the displayed Web page but all Web pages on a Web site. Look for a Search text box and make sure that it searches the site — and not the entire Internet.

Figure 7-5: The Find dialog box

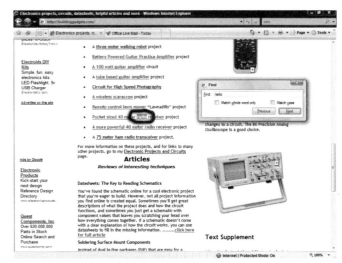

Figure 7-6: A found word highlighted on a Web page

Set Up a Home Page

1. Open IE and choose Tools⇨Internet Options.

2. In the resulting Internet Options dialog box, on the General tab, enter a Web site address to use as your home page, as shown in Figure 7-7. Note that you can enter several home pages that will appear on different tabs every time you open IE, as shown in Figure 7-8.

   Alternatively, click one of the following preset option buttons, as shown in Figure 7-7:

   - **Use Current:** Sets whatever page is currently displayed in the browser window as your home page.

   - **Use Default:** This setting sends you to the MSN Web page.

   - **Use Blank:** If you're a minimalist, this setting is for you. No Web page displays; you just see a blank area.

3. Click OK.

4. Click the Home Page icon to go to your home page.

 If you want to have more than one home page, you can create multiple home page tabs that will display when you click the Home button. Click the arrow on the Home button and choose Add or Change Home Page. In the Add or Change Home Page dialog box that appears, click the Add this page to your home page tabs radio button, and then click Yes. Display other sites and repeat this procedure for all the home page tabs you want.

 To remove a home page you have set up, click the arrow on the Home Page button and choose Remove and then choose a particular home page, or choose Remove All from the sub menu that appears.

Figure 7-7: The Internet Options dialog box

Figure 7-8: Two home page tabs

Add a Web Site to Favorites

1. Open IE, enter the URL of a Web site that you want to add to your Favorites list, and then click Go (the button with blue arrows on it to the right of the Address bar.

2. Click the Add to Favorites button and then choose Add to Favorites.

3. In the resulting Favorites Center dialog box, as shown in Figure 7-9, modify the name of the Favorite listing to something easily recognizable. If you wish, choose another folder or create a folder to store the Favorite in.

4. Click Add to add the site.

5. Click the Favorites Center button and then click the name of the site from the list that's displayed (see Figure 7-10) to go to that site.

 Regularly cleaning out your Favorites list is a good idea — after all, do you really need the sites that you used to plan last year's vacation? With the Favorites Center displayed, right-click any item and then choose Delete or Rename to modify the favorite listing.

 You can keep the Favorites Center as a side pane in Internet Explorer by displaying it and then clicking the Pin the Favorites Center button (it has a left-facing green arrow on it and is located to the right of the History button).

Figure 7-9: The Favorites Center dialog box

Figure 7-10: Favorites Web sites displayed in the Favorites pane

Organize Favorites

1. With Internet Explorer open, click the Add to Favorites button and then choose Organize Favorites.

2. In the resulting Organize Favorites dialog box (see Figure 7-11), click the New Folder, Move, Rename, or Delete buttons to organize your favorites.

3. When you finish organizing your Favorites, click Close.

 These steps provide a handy way to manage several sites or folders, but you can also organize favorite sites one by one by using the Favorites pane. (You display the Favorites pane by clicking the Favorites button.) Right-click any favorite site listed in the pane and choose a command: Create New Folder, Delete, Rename, or Sort by Name, for example.

 If you create new folders in the above steps, then you will have to manually transfer files into those folders. To do this just display the Favorites Center and click and drag files listed there on top of folders.

Figure 7-11: Organize Favorites dialog box

Work with Tabs

1. With Internet Explorer open, click New Tab (the smallest tab on the far right of the tabs).

2. A new tab appears, which displays some information about tabs (see Figure 7-12). Enter a URL in the Address bar. The URL opens in that tab. You can then click other tabs to switch among sites.

3. Click the Quicktabs button (it consists of four little squares on the far left of the tabs) to display a thumbnail of all open tabs (see Figure 7-13), or click the Tab List button (the arrow to the right of the Quicktabs button) to display a text list of tabs.

4. Close an active tab by clicking the Close button on the right.

 A *tab* is a sort of window you can use to view any number of sites. You don't have to create a new tab to go to another site. Having the ability to keep a few tabs open at a time means you can more quickly switch between two or more sites without navigating back and forth either with the Previous or Next buttons or by entering URLs. You can also create more than one Home Page tab that can appear every time you open IE. See the task "Set Up a Home Page" for more about this.

 You can also press Ctrl+T to open a new tab in Internet Explorer. Also, if you want to keep one tab open and close all others, right-click the tab you want to keep open and choose Close Other Tabs.

Figure 7-12: A newly created tab

Figure 7-13: Quicktabs displaying thumbnails of all open tabs

View Your Browsing History

1. Click the Favorites Center button and then click History to display the History pane (see Figure 7-14).

2. Click the down-arrow on the History button (see Figure 7-15) and select a sort method:

   - **By Date:** Sort favorites by date visited.

   - **By Site:** Sort alphabetically by site name.

   - **By Most Visited:** Sort with the sites visited most on top and those visited least at the bottom of the list.

   - **By Order Visited Today:** Sort by the order in which you visited sites today.

3. In the History pane, you can click a site to go to it. The History pane closes.

 You can also choose the arrow on the right of the Address bar to display sites you've visited.

 Choose Search History on the History menu to display a search box you can use to search for sites you've visited.

Figure 7-14: The History pane

Figure 7-15: The History sort menu

Customize the Internet Explorer Toolbar

1. Open IE.

2. Click Tools⇨Toolbars⇨Customize. The Customize Toolbar dialog box (as shown in Figure 7-16) appears.

3. Click a tool on the left and then click the Add button to add it to the toolbar.

4. Click a tool on the right and then click the Remove button to remove it from the toolbar.

5. When you're finished, click Close to save your new toolbar settings. The new tools appear (see Figure 7-17); click the double-arrow button on the right of the toolbar to display any tools that IE can't fit onscreen.

 You can use the Move Up and Move Down buttons in the Customize Toolbar dialog box to rearrange the order in which tools appear on the toolbar. To reset the toolbar to defaults, click the Reset button in that same dialog box.

 If you want to add some space between tools on the toolbar so they're easier to see, click the Separator item in the Available Toolbar Buttons list and add it before or after a tool button.

Figure 7-16: The Customize Toolbar dialog box

Figure 7-17: Display any additional tools by clicking the button on the right of the toolbar

Download Files

1. Open a Web site that contains downloadable files. Typically Web sites offer a Download button or link that initiates a file download.

2. Click the appropriate link to proceed. Windows Vista might display a dialog box asking your permission to proceed with the download; click Yes.

3. In the resulting File Download dialog box, as shown in Figure 7-18, choose either option:

    -   **Click Run to download to a temporary folder.** You can run an installation program for software, for example. However, beware: If you run a program directly from the Internet, you could be introducing dangerous viruses to your system. You might want to set up an antivirus program to scan files before downloading them.

    -   **Click Save to save the file to your hard drive.** In the Save As dialog box, select the folder on your computer or removable storage media (a CD-ROM, for example) where you want to save the file. If you're downloading software, you need to locate the downloaded file and click it to run the installation.

         If you're worried that a particular file might be unsafe to download (for example, if it's from an unknown source and, being an executable file type, could contain a virus), click Cancel in the File Download dialog box.

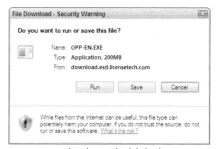

Figure 7-18: The File Download dialog box

 If a particular file will take a long time to download (the Windows Vista beta version took me over 20 hours!) you may have to babysit it. If your computer goes into standby it could pause the download. If your computer automatically downloads updates it may cause your computer to restart automatically as well, cancelling or halting your download. Check in periodically to keep things moving along.

Change Privacy Settings

1. With IE open, choose Tools⇨Internet Options and click the Privacy tab, as shown in Figure 7-19.

2. Click the slider and drag it up or down to make different levels of security settings.

3. Read the choices and select a setting that suits you.

4. Click the Sites button to specify sites to always or never allow the use of cookies. In the resulting Per Site Privacy Actions dialog box (as shown in Figure 7-20), enter a site in the Address of Website box and click either Block or Allow.

5. Click OK twice to save your new settings.

 The default setting, Medium, is probably a good bet for most people. To restore the default setting, click the Default button in the Internet Options dialog box Privacy tab or use the slider to move back to Medium.

 You can also use pop-up blocker settings on the Privacy tab to specify which pop-up windows to allow or block. Just click the Settings button, enter a Web site name, and then click Add to allow pop-ups.

Figure 7-19: The Privacy tab of the Internet Options dialog box

Figure 7-20: The Per Site Privacy Actions dialog box

Enable the Content Advisor

1. With IE open, choose Tools⇨Internet Options.

2. In the resulting Internet Options dialog box, click the Content tab to display it.

3. Click the Enable button. (*Note:* If there is no Enable button but Disable and Settings buttons instead, Content Advisor is already enabled. Click the Settings button to see the options and make changes if you wish.)

4. On the Ratings tab of the Content Advisor dialog box (see Figure 7-21), click one of the categories (such as Depiction of Drug Use) and then move the slider to use one of three site screening settings: None, Limited, or Unrestricted.

5. Repeat Step 4 for each of the categories.

6. Click the Approved Sites tab (see Figure 7-22) and enter the name of a specific site that you want to control access to. Then click Always or Never.

   - **Always** allows users to view the site, even if it's included in the Content Advisor screening level you've set.

   - **Never** means that nobody can visit the site even if it's acceptable to Content Advisor.

7. When you finish making your settings, click OK twice to save them.

 If you want to view sites that you don't want others to see, you can do that, too. On the General tab of the Content Advisor dialog box, make sure that the Supervisor Can Type a Password to Allow Viewers to View Restricted Content check box is selected, and then click Create Password. In the dialog box that appears, enter the password, confirm it, and then enter a hint and click OK. Now if you're logged on as the system administrator, you can get to any restricted site by using this password.

Figure 7-21: The Ratings tab of the Content Advisor dialog box

Figure 7-22: The Approved Sites tab of the Content Advisor

View RSS Feeds

1. Click the Favorites Center button; then click the Feeds button to display a list of recently displayed RSS Feeds (see Figure 7-23).

2. Click a Feed to display it (see Figure 7-24).

3. You can also click the View Feeds on This Page button on the toolbar to view any active feeds listed on the currently displayed page.

 The View Feeds on This Page button is grayed out when there are no RSS feeds on the current page, and it turns Red when feeds are present.

 Though Internet Explorer has an RSS feed reader built in, you can explore other feed readers. Just type "RSS feeds" into Internet Explorer's Search box to find more information and listings of readers and RSS feed sites.

Figure 7-23: The RSS Feeds pane

Figure 7-24: An RSS Feed site

Print a Web Page

1. If a Web page includes a link or button to print or display a print version of a page, click that and follow the instructions.

2. If the page doesn't include a link for printing, click the Print button on the IE toolbar.

3. In the resulting Print dialog box, decide how much of the document you want to print and then select one of the options in the Page Range area, as shown in Figure 7-25.

 Note that choosing Current Page or entering page numbers in the Pages text box of the Print dialog box doesn't mean much when printing a Web page — the whole document might print because Web pages aren't divided into pages as word processing documents are.

4. Click the up arrow in the Number of Copies text box to print multiple copies. If you want multiple copies collated, select the Collate check box.

5. When you adjust all settings you need, click Print.

Figure 7-25: The Print dialog box

Exchanging E-Mail with Windows Mail

*O*nce upon a time, people chatted around the water cooler or over lunch, but that's all changed now. Now the place to spend your time communicating is online.

Although instant messaging from your cell phone is all the rage, e-mail is still the cornerstone of online communication. You've probably sent an e-mail (unless you were brought up by wolves in the forest), but you might not be familiar with the ins and outs of using *Windows Mail*, the e-mail program from Microsoft that's built into Windows Vista.

To make your e-mailing life easy, this chapter takes a look at these tasks:

- **Receive, send, and forward messages.** Deal with the ins and outs of receiving and sending e-mail. Use the formatting tools that Windows Mail provides to make your messages more attractive and readable.

- **Add information into the Address Book.** You can quickly and easily manage your contacts as well as organize the messages you save in e-mail folders.

- **Set up the layout of all Windows Mail features.** Use the Folder bar and Layout features to create the most efficient workspace.

- **Manage your e-mail account.** Set up an e-mail account, and then create, modify, and add rules for your account to operate by.

Chapter

8

Get ready to . . .

Open Windows Mail and Receive Messages

1. Choose Start⇨All Programs⇨Windows Mail.

2. In the Windows Mail window, press Ctrl+M to send and receive all messages.

3. Click the Inbox item in the Folders list to view messages. New messages sport a small closed envelope icon; those with attachments have a paper clip icon as well (see Figure 8-1).

 To organize messages in the Inbox, click any of the headings at the top, such as From (to sort the messages alphabetically by sender), Received (to sort by the date they were received), and so on.

 If your mail doesn't come through it's probably because your e-mail provider's servers are experiencing technical problems. Just wait a little while and try to retrieve your mail again. If you still can't get mail (and you know you should have received some by now) contact your e-mail provider to find out what the problem is and when it will be fixed.

 Note that if an e-mail has a little exclamation point to the left of it in your Inbox somebody has flagged it as urgent. It's usually best to check out those e-mails first!

Figure 8-1: The Windows Mail Inbox

Manage an E-Mail Account

1. In the Windows Mail main window, choose Tools⇨ Accounts.

2. In the resulting Internet Accounts dialog box, as shown in Figure 8-2, do any of the following:

- To remove an account, click the Remove button on any of the tabs. A confirming message appears. To delete the account, click Yes.

- Select an account and click the Set as Default button to make it the account that Windows connects you to when you go online. In the case of the mail server, the default is the one used to send any message.

3. To set up a new account, click Add.

4. In the resulting Internet Connection Wizard (see Figure 8-3), choose an account type: E-mail, Newsgroup, or Directory Service for online search services used by the Contacts feature to search for people.

5. Click Next. In the following screen, follow the set-up instructions.

 Following the Internet Connection Wizard often requires that you provide certain information about your Internet service provider (ISP), such as its mail server or connection method. Keep this information handy!

6. When you finish setting up accounts, click the Close button to close the Internet Accounts dialog box.

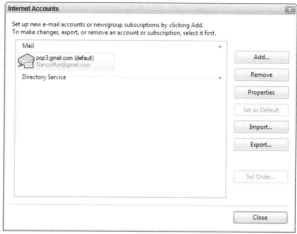

Figure 8-2: The Internet Accounts dialog box

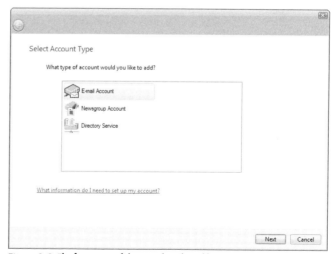

Figure 8-3: The first screen of the wizard used to add an account

Create and Send E-Mail

1. Choose Start➪All Programs➪Windows Mail.

2. Click the Create Mail button on the Windows Mail toolbar to create a new blank e-mail form (see Figure 8-4).

3. Type the e-mail address of the recipient in the To field text box and an address in the Cc field text box to send a copy of the message.

4. Click in the Subject field text box and type a concise yet descriptive subject.

5. Click in the message window and type your message (see Figure 8-5).

 Don't press Enter at the end of a line. Windows Mail has an automatic text wrap feature that does this for you. Also, keep e-mail etiquette in mind as you type. For example, don't type in ALL CAPITAL LETTERS. This is called *shouting*, which is considered rude.

 Do be polite even if you're really, really angry. Your message could be forwarded to just about anybody, just about anywhere, and you don't want to get a reputation as a hothead. Do be concise. If you have lots to say, consider sending a letter by snail-mail or overnight delivery. Most people tire of reading text onscreen after a short while.

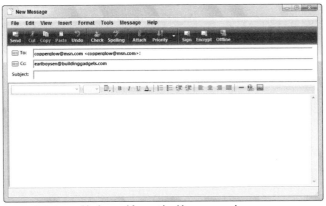

Figure 8-4: A new, blank e-mail form with addresses entered

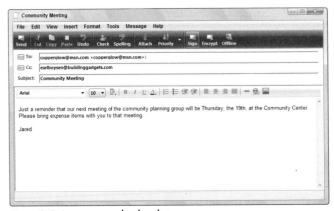

Figure 8-5: A message typed and ready to go

6. When you finish typing your message, spell-check it (unless you're the regional state spelling champ). Click the Spelling button; possibly misspelled words get highlighted, and the Spelling dialog box appears (see Figure 8-6). At this point, you have some choices:

- Click the Ignore button to ignore this instance of the misspelling.

- Click the Ignore All button to ignore all instances.

- Choose a suggested alternate spelling and click the Change button to change that instance; or, click the Change All button to change all instances of the word.

- Click the Add button to add the current spelling of the word to the Spelling feature dictionary so it's never questioned again.

7. Click the Close button to close the Spelling Checker. Click the Send button. The message is on its way!

 If the message is really urgent, you might also click the Priority button to add a bright red exclamation mark to the message header to alert the recipient. Click twice again to return the priority to Low.

Figure 8-6: The Spelling dialog box

 Remember that when creating an e-mail, you can address it to a stored address by using the Address Book feature. Click the To button, and your Address Book appears. You can then select a contact from there. Windows Mail also allows you to just begin to type a stored contact in an address field (To or Cc), and it fills in likely options while you type. When it fills in the correct name, just press Enter to select it.

Send an Attachment

1. Create a new e-mail message, address it, and enter a subject.

2. Click the Attach File to Message button.

3. In Open dialog box that appears (see Figure 8-7), locate the file that you want and then click Open.

4. With the name of the attached file now in the Attach field text box (see Figure 8-8), type a message (or not — after all, a picture *is* worth a thousand words).

5. Click the Send button to send.

 If you want to send somebody your own contact information, create a business card in your Address Book and attach it to an e-mail. This is saved in *vCard format*, and the recipient can then import it into his or her Address Book. Just create yourself as a contact. Then, in the Address Book window, right-click the contact and choose Send Contact (vCard). A blank e-mail opens with the card attached.

 Some e-mail programs limit the time that the program attempts to get mail from your server. If you sometimes get a message that your connection timed out, choose Tools⊃Accounts, select your e-mail account, and then click Properties. On the Advanced tab, move the Server Timeout slider a bit to the right to allow for a longer time period before timing out.

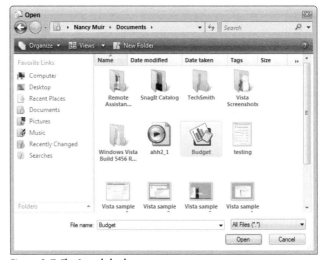

Figure 8-7: The Open dialog box

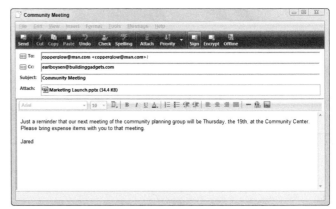

Figure 8-8: The Attach field showing an attached file

Read a Message

1. Click an e-mail message in your Inbox or double-click it to open it in a separate window. Unread messages sport an icon of an unopened envelope to the left of the message subject.

2. Use the scrollbars in the message window to scroll down through the message and read it (see Figure 8-9).

3. If the message has an attachment, it shows a paper clip symbol when the message is closed in your Inbox; attachments are listed in the Attach box in the open message. To open an attachment, double-click it.

4. In the Mail Attachment dialog box (see Figure 8-10), click the Open button. The attachment opens in whatever program is associated with it (such as the Windows Fax and Picture Viewer for a graphics file) or the program it was created in (such as Word for Windows).

 If you'd rather save an attachment to a storage disk or your hard drive, right-click the attachment name in the Attach field and choose Save As. In the Save As dialog box that appears, choose a location and provide a name for the file; then click Save.

Figure 8-9: A newly received e-mail message

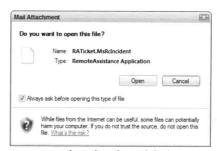

Figure 8-10: The Mail Attachment dialog box

Reply to a Message

1. Open the message you want to reply to, and then select one of the following reply options, as shown in Figure 8-11:

   • **Reply:** Send the reply to only the author.

   • **Reply All:** Send a reply to the author as well as everyone who received the original message.

2. In the resulting e-mail form (see Figure 8-12), enter any additional recipient(s) in the To and/or Cc text boxes and type your message in the message window area.

3. Click the Send button to send the reply.

 If you don't want to include the original message in your reply, choose Tools⇨Options and click the Send tab. Clear the Include Message in Reply check box, and then click OK.

Forward E-Mail

1. Open the e-mail message that you want to forward.

2. Click the Forward button on the toolbar.

3. In the message that appears with Fw added to the beginning of the subject line, enter a new recipient(s) in the To and Cc fields, and then enter any message that you want to include in the message window area, as shown in the example in Figure 8-12.

4. Click Send to forward the message.

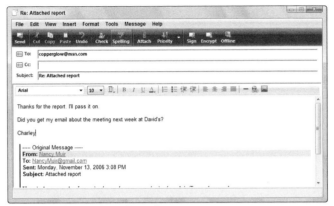

Figure 8-11: Reply to the sender or all recipients

Figure 8-12: A message ready to be sent

Create and Add a Signature

1. Choose Tools⇨Options to open the Options dialog box. Click the Signatures tab (see Figure 8-13).

2. Click the New button to create a new signature and then enter your Signatures text.

3. Select the Add Signatures to All Outgoing Messages check box and make sure that the signature is selected as the default. (*Note:* Select the Don't Add Signatures to Replies and Forwards check box if you want to add your signature only occasionally.)

4. Click OK to save the signature. To manually add a signature to an open e-mail message with the message open, choose Insert⇨Signature and select a signature from the list that appears to insert it (see Figure 8-14).

 If you have different e-mail accounts and want to assign a different signature to each one, go to the Signatures tab of the Options dialog box. There, select a signature in the Signatures list box, click the Advanced button, and then select an account to associate it with.

 Remember that if you attach your signature to every outgoing e-mail including e-mail replies, whoever you communicate with will get the information provided there. Consider issues of identity theft before you provide your address, phone number, and other personal information to all and sundry.

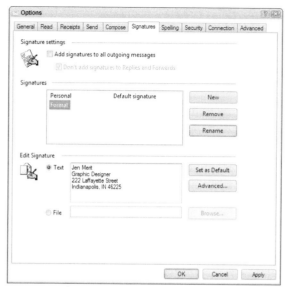

Figure 8-13: The Options dialog box, Signatures tab

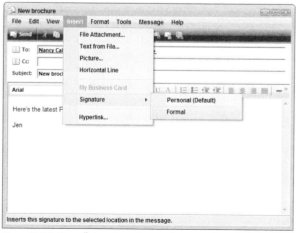

Figure 8-14: Manually inserting a signature in an e-mail

Format E-Mail Messages

1. Create a new e-mail message or open a message and click Reply or Forward.

2. Select the text that you want to format (see Figure 8-15).

3. Use any of the following options to make changes to the font. (See the toolbar containing these tools in Figure 8-16 and a message with various formats applied.)

   - **Font drop-down list:** Choose an option from the drop-down list to apply it to the text.

   - **Font Size drop-down list:** Change the font size here.

   - **Paragraph Style button:** Apply a preset style, such as Heading 1 or Address.

   - **Bold, Italic, or Underline buttons:** Apply styles to selected text.

   - **Font Color button:** Display a color palette and click a color to apply it to selected text.

   - **Formatting Numbers or Formatting Bullets buttons:** Apply numbering order to lists or precede each item with a round bullet.

   - **Increase Indentation or Decrease Indentation button:** Indent that paragraph to the right or move (decrease) it to the left.

   - **Align Left, Center, Align Right, or Justify buttons:** Adjust the alignment.

   - **Insert Horizontal Line button:** Add a line to your message.

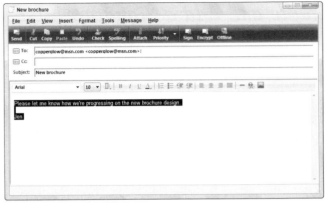

Figure 8-15: Text selected for formatting

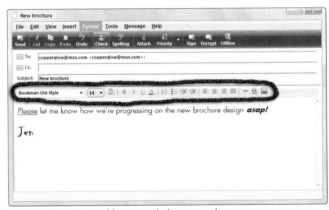

Figure 8-16: A variety of formats applied to an e-mail message

Add Stationery

1. Click the arrow on the Create Mail button in the Windows Mail main window and select a stationery option listed in the menu that appears, or choose the Select Stationery command to get more choices.

2. In the Select Stationery dialog box that appears (see Figure 8-17), select a stationery from the list.

3. Click OK to apply the stationery to the new message.

4. With a new, reply, or forwarded message open, you can apply stationery using either of these methods:

   • Choose Format⇨Apply Stationery, and then click a stationery to apply (see Figure 8-18).

   • Choose More Stationery to access the Select Stationery dialog box.

 You can also insert a picture in an e-mail. With the e-mail form open, choose Insert⇨Picture. Locate a picture in the Picture window that appears and click Open. The picture fills the background of the e-mail message area.

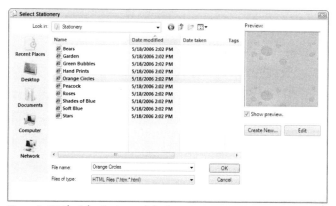

Figure 8-17: The Select Stationery dialog box

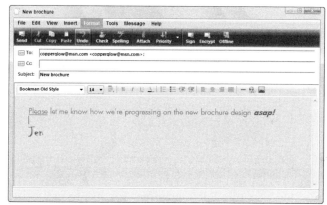

Figure 8-18: Stationery applied to an e-mail message

Add Contacts to the Address Book

1. In the Windows Mail main window, click the Contacts button to open the Contacts window.

2. To create a new contact in the resulting Contacts window, as shown in Figure 8-19, right-click on a name and choose New➪Contact. (*Note:* New Contact Group can be used to create a group of people from existing contacts, such as your car pool members.)

3. In the resulting Properties dialog box, as shown in Figure 8-20, go to the following options tabs to enter contact information:

   - **Name and E-mail tab:** Enter the person's name and e-mail address. (This is the only information you must enter to create a contact.)

   - **Home tab:** Enter the person's home and Web site addresses as well as phone, fax, and cellphone numbers.

   - **Work tab:** Enter information about the company that the person works for as well as his job title and pager number. You can even add a map to help you find his office.

   - **Family tab:** Enter the person's family members' names, as well as his or her gender, birthday, and anniversary.

   - **Notes tab:** Enter any notes you like to in the form on this tab.

   - **IDs tab:** Ensure secure communications. *Digital IDs* are certificates that you can use to verify the identity of the person with whom you're communicating.

4. Click OK to save your new contact information, and then close the Contacts window.

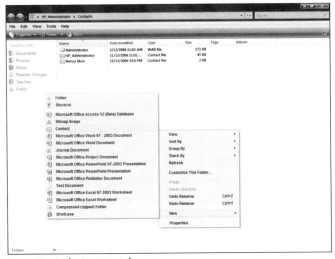

Figure 8-19: The Contacts window

Figure 8-20: The Properties dialog box (Add text)

Customize the Windows Mail Layout

1. Choose View➪Layout to open the Window Layout Properties dialog box.

2. Select various check boxes in the Basic section, as shown in Figure 8-21, to select items to display in separate panes (see Figure 8-22), including

- **Folder List:** A pane containing a list of all folders.

- **Folder Bar:** A bar near the top of the screen that includes a drop-down list of folders.

- **Toolbar:** The bar containing tools you use to create and work with messages, such as Create, Reply, Forward, and Print.

- **Status Bar:** The bar across the bottom of screen that lists the number of messages in all your folders and the number of unread messages.

- **Views Bar:** A bar under the toolbar containing a drop-down menu with three commands: Hide Read Messages, Hide Read or Ignored Messages, and Show All Messages.

- **Search Bar:** The bar that allows you to search your mail for keywords or other criteria.

3. Select various options in the Preview Pane section to preview a message selected in the Inbox, Outbox, Drafts, Sent Items, or Deleted Items folders.

4. Click OK to apply and save all your layout settings.

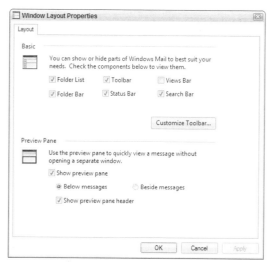

Figure 8-21: The Layout Properties dialog box

Figure 8-22: Various elements displayed in Windows Mail

Create Message Folders

1. Choose View⇨Layout to open the Window Layout Properties dialog box.

2. Select check boxes to display the Folders list and Folder bar and then click OK.

3. In the Folders list, click any folder to display its contents (see Figure 8-23).

4. Choose File⇨Folder⇨New.

5. In the resulting Create Folder dialog box (see Figure 8-24), select the folder that you want the new folder to be created in and then enter a new folder name.

6. Click OK.

 Typically, you select the Local Folders item in Step 5 so that the new folder is at the same level as the Inbox, Outbox, and so on. Alternatively, you could select the Inbox item to place the new folder within the Inbox folder.

Figure 8-23: The Folders list in the Windows Mail Folder bar

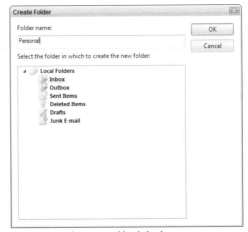

Figure 8-24: The Create Folder dialog box

Organize Messages in Folders

1. In the Folders list, click an arrow symbol to the left of any folder to display its contents (see Figure 8-25).

2. To place a message in a folder, you can do one of these actions:

   - With a folder (such as the Inbox) displayed, click a message and then drag it into a folder in the Folders list.

   - With an e-mail message open, choose File⊃Move to Folder or Copy to Folder. In the dialog box that appears (see Figure 8-26), select the appropriate folder and click OK.

   - Right-click a message in a displayed folder and choose Move to Folder or Copy to Folder. In the dialog box that appears, select the appropriate folder and then click OK.

3. To delete a message, display the folder it's saved to, select it, and then click the Delete button or press Delete (on your keyboard).

 If you try to delete a message from your Deleted Items folder, a message appears asking whether you really want to delete this message permanently. That's because when you delete a message from another folder, it's really not deleted; instead, it's simply placed in the Deleted Items folder. To send it into oblivion, you have to delete it from the Deleted Items folder, confirming your deletion so that Windows Mail is really convinced that you mean what you say.

Figure 8-25: The Folders list, which you find in the Windows Mail Folder Bar

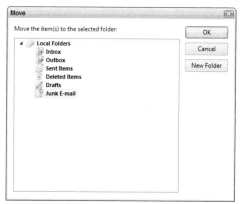

Figure 8-26: The Move dialog box

Create Mail Rules

1. Choose Tools➪Message Rules➪Mail.

2. In the resulting New Mail Rule dialog box (see Figure 8-27), select the check box to set a Condition for the rule. For example, if you want all messages that contain the word *Sale* in the subject line to be moved to a Junk Mail folder, select the Where the Subject Line Contains Specific Words option.

3. Select the Select the Actions for Your Rule check boxes to choose rule actions. In the example in Step 2, for instance, you would select the Move It to the Specified Folder option.

4. In the Rule Description area, click a link (the colored text). To continue the example shown in Figure 8-27, you click the phrase Contains Specific Words. Fill in the specific information for the rule in the dialog box that appears (see Figure 8-28 for an example). For the second item in this example, click the word specified and select a folder for matching messages to be moved to.

5. Click OK to save the description and return to the New Mail Rule dialog box. Fill in the Name of the Rule text box with a name that you can recognize, and then click OK.

After you create a rule, open the Message Rules dialog box (choose Tools➪Message Rules➪Mail) and then click the Modify button in the Message dialog box to make changes to the rule, or click the Remove button to delete it.

Here are some rules that people find handy to create: Place messages marked as priority in a Priority folder, or put messages with attachments in an Attachments folder. When you're on vacation, choose to have all messages forwarded to somebody else, such as an assistant; or, if a message is from a certain person, mark it with a color. **Note:** If you use the autoforward feature, you have to leave your computer on and also leave Windows Mail open while you're away.

Figure 8-27: The New Mail Rule dialog box with rule information selected

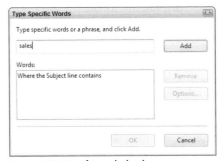

Figure 8-28: Specifying rule details

Working Remotely

We live in a hurry-up-and-go society. Gone are the days when you could sit back during your flight from Des Moines to Chicago and take a snooze. These days, people do as much work in the air and on the road as in cubicles and offices.

Windows Vista hasn't left the road warrior behind: It offers several features that help keep you in touch and help you connect your Windows computer to mobile devices, such as a personal digital assistant (PDA) or cellphone.

The Windows Vista remote control features include

➡ Power management tools called *Power Plans* for laptops to make sure that you don't run out of juice at an all-important moment.

➡ The ability to connect to a wireless network, such as the kind you find in airports, restaurants, and hotels.

➡ A feature that lets you send documents on your computer over a phone line to a fax machine.

➡ Features to let your modem dial from a remote location by setting up a different originating location than your home or office, and even dial by using a calling card for long distance calls.

Chapter 9

Get ready to . . .

Create a Power Plan for a Laptop

1. Choose Start⇨Control Panel⇨System and Maintenance, and then click the Power Options link.

2. In the Select a Power Plan window, as shown in Figure 9-1, select a scheme. Power Saver is a good option for a laptop computer.

3. To change settings, click the Change Plan Settings link under any Power Plan. In the window that displays (see Figure 9-2), click the arrow and choose another setting for the length of time of inactivity before the display shuts off to save power.

4. Click the Save Changes button to save the settings and then click the Close button to close the Control Panel.

 In the window for changing plan settings, you can click the Change Advanced Power Settings link to modify such settings as requiring a password to wake up your computer, when to turn off your hard disk, or when to automatically go into hibernation mode.

 There are trade-offs to make in power plan settings. For example, if you have your computer go into hibernation after a very short time, it may help you save battery power, but, depending on your settings, you may have to log into Windows again each time you revive it. See Chaper 14 for information about how to modify user accounts and password settings to make getting back to work as quick as possible.

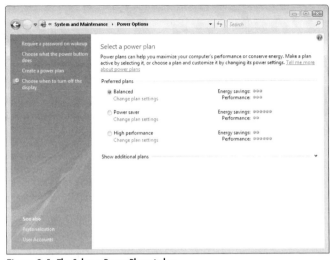

Figure 9-1: The Select a Power Plan window

Figure 9-2: Changing power plan settings

Create a Custom Power Plan

1. Choose Start⇨Control Panel, and then click the Power Options link.

2. In the Power Options window, click the Create a Power Plan link.

3. In the Create a Power Plan window (see Figure 9-3), select the plan that is close to what you want to create, enter the name for your plan in the Plan Name field, and then click Next.

4. In the Edit Plan Settings window that appears, click the arrow to display a drop-down list of timings for turning off the display and then choose one.

5. Click the Create button to add the plan to your list of Power Plans.

If you create a plan, there are no Energy Savings or Performance ratings next to it in the plan list. Also, if you make changes to an existing plan, those ratings don't change. If somebody else will use the computer, either let him know about this or reset the plans to default to avoid confusion. (In the Change Plan Settings window, select Restore Default Settings for this Plan.)

Connect to a Wireless Network

1. With the Windows Vista taskbar displayed, right-click the Network icon on the taskbar.

2. Click Connect to a Network. The Connect to a Network window appears (see Figure 9-4).

3. Click a network to select it and then click Connect. Windows Vista checks the connection and connects you.

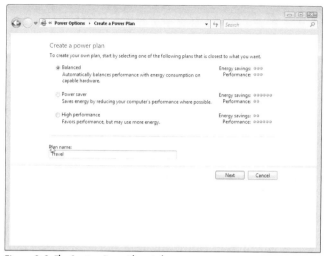

Figure 9-3: The Create a Power Plan window

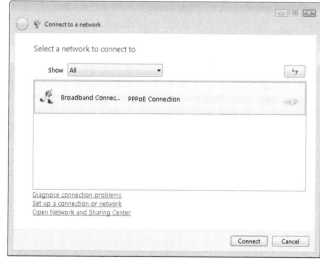

Figure 9-4: The Connect to a Network window

Send a Fax from Your Computer

1. Be sure that you connected your computer to a phone line, and then choose Start➪All Programs➪Windows Fax and Scan.

2. In the Windows Fax and Scan window that appears (see Figure 9-5), click the New Fax button. If you haven't set up the Fax feature, the Fax Setup Wizard appears. Click Connect to a Fax Modem and then follow instructions to set up the connection.

3. When you finish the setup wizard, a new fax cover page form (see Figure 9-6) is displayed.

4. Enter the recipient's information (this must be a contact you have saved with a fax number) and subject, as well as any message you want to include. Click Insert to add a file or pages from a scanner in your message.

5. Click Send to send the fax.

 These days there are several alternatives to faxing. If you have a scanner you can scan images into your computer and then send them as attachments to e-mail, which is covered in Chapter 8. You can also use a document reader program such as Adobe to save a document as a PDF file. Anybody who has Adobe, which is free, can open that file and view the document without having to have the originating software available to them. If the person you're trying to communicate with can't receive a fax, consider these two options.

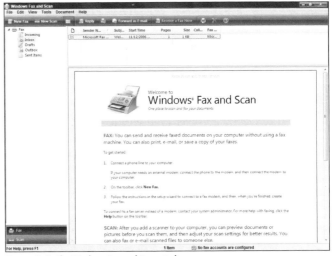

Figure 9-5: The Windows Fax and Scan window

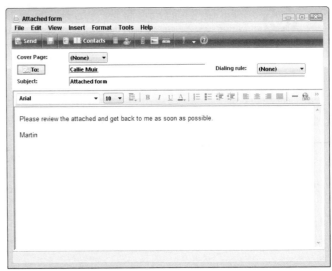

Figure 9-6: A fax form

Set Up Long Distance Dialing away from Home

1. Choose Start⇨Control Panel, click the Hardware and Sound link, and then click the Phone and Modem Options link.

2. Click New. In the New Location dialog box, as shown in Figure 9-7, click the arrow on the Country/Region drop-down list and choose a location.

3. Enter your area code and any other information you need to access a carrier or reach an outside line; then click OK.

4. In the Phone and Modem Options dialog box that appears (see Figure 9-8), click OK to save your settings.

 If you're in a remote location, say at the North Pole, and need to use a different telephony provider in a certain location, you can click the Advanced tab of the Phone and Modem Options dialog box to choose an option or add another carrier. For example, people often use a TAPI (Telephony Application Programming Interface) provider for setting up an application to access a server's voice service to handle multicast conferencing. (If you don't know what multicast conferencing is, you'll probably never need this setting.)

 Keep in mind that most ISPs can provide you with a local access number so you don't have to dial long distance to access your Internet account. It's a good idea to look this number up on your ISP's Web site before you travel so you don't have spend money connecting remotely just to get the local number!

Figure 9-7: The New Location dialog box

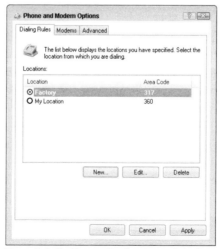

Figure 9-8: The Phone and Modem Options dialog box

Set Up a Calling Card

1. Choose Start⇨Control Panel, click the Hardware and Sound link, and then click the Phone and Modem Options link.

2. In the Phone and Modem Options dialog box (shown in Figure 9-9), select an option from the Location list box, and then click the Edit button.

3. In the Edit Location dialog box that appears, click the Calling Card tab (as shown in Figure 9-10).

4. Select an option from the Card Types list box.

5. Enter the calling card number in the Account Number text box and then enter the PIN in the Personal ID Number text box.

6. Click OK to save the settings.

 If you have a calling card that isn't listed in the Card Types list box on the Calling Card tab, leave the default setting of None, and then click the New button to enter information about your specific calling card.

 If you have a problem when your modem dials a number, you might need to specify a rule for accessing an outline line. On the General tab of the Edit Location dialog box, make an entry in the To Access An Outline Line for Local (or Long Distance) Calls box to fix this problem.

Figure 9-9: The Phone and Modem Options dialog box

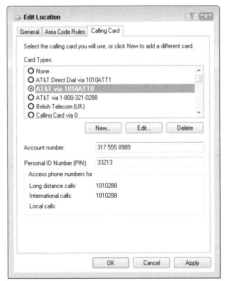

Figure 9-10: The Edit Location dialog box, Calling Card tab

Make a Dialup Connection by Using an Infrared-Enabled Cellular Phone

1. If necessary, check with your phone manufacturer or documentation to make sure that your cellphone's infrared feature is turned on.

2. Line up the infrared transceiver on your phone and the transceiver on your computer within a few feet of each other.

3. Choose Start⇨Network.

4. In the Network window, click the Network and Sharing Center link.

5. In the Network and Sharing Center window (as shown in Figure 9-11), click the Set Up a Connection or Network link.

6. In the Choose a Connection Option window, as shown in Figure 9-12, click any of the four connection types, depending on what kind of connection you want to set up.

7. Continue with the various wizard settings. When you finish the wizard, you should be able to connect to this location by using your cellular phone, as long as your phone and computer are aligned properly.

 If you're not sure whether your computer or laptop supports infrared connections, look for a small, dark red window on the computer or laptop case (that's the infrared transceiver; it looks like a similar window on your TV remote control), or check your device documentation. You can also go to the Device Manager through the Control Panel and look under Infrared Devices to see whether any are listed.

 For more about the specifics of using your cell phone with a wireless network connection, check your phone manufacturer's user manual.

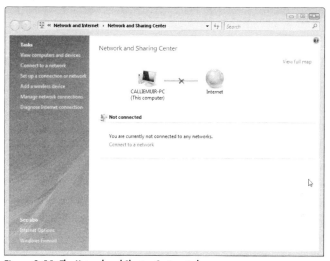

Figure 9-11: The Network and Sharing Center window

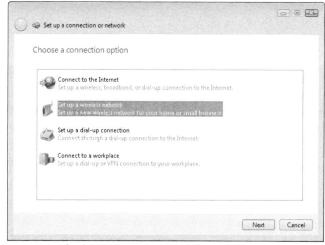

Figure 9-12: The Choose a Connection Option window of the New Connection Wizard

Part III
Setting Up Hardware and Networks

The 5th Wave   By Rich Tennant

"I really think the Home Basic version will work fine for you. Besides, there is no Yurt Basic version of Vista."

Setting Up New Hardware

*P*eripherals, graphics cards, modems, SCSI (pronounced *skuz*-zee, if you please) — just what the heck is all this stuff?

Collectively, these items belong to the category of *computer hardware.* Your CPU and monitor are hardware. So are the cards slotted into your CPU that provide memory to run software and the mechanisms for playing sounds and videos. Printers are hardware, as is anything else that plugs into your computer.

Installing a new piece of hardware used to be a great occasion for groaning and moaning. Nothing was compatible, everything installed differently, and Windows itself didn't have much in the way of popular *drivers* (software that runs various pieces of hardware) ready and waiting. That all changed with a technology called *Plug and Play,* which automates the installation process and some standardizing of connections through Universal Serial Bus (USB) ports. Windows Vista now comes with a full framework of drivers for hardware devices, and whatever it doesn't have is usually easy to download from any hardware manufacturer's Web site. In this chapter, you find out how you can

➥ **Install and set up common peripherals.** Peripherals include a monitor, printer, and modem.

➥ **Install and set up cards that slot into your CPU; partition your hard drive.** Add sound and video; also, add hard drive partitions to optimize memory.

Get ready to . . .

Install a Printer

1. Read the instructions that came with the printer. Some printers require that you install software before connecting them, but others can be connected right away.

2. Turn on your computer and then follow the option that fits your needs:

   • If your printer is a Plug and Play device, connect it; Windows Vista installs what it needs automatically.

   • Insert the disk/c that came with the device and follow the onscreen instructions.

   • Choose Start↵Control Panel↵Printer (under the Hardware and Sound category); in the window that appears, click Add A Printer. If this is the option that you're following, proceed to the next step in this list.

3. If you choose the third option in Step 2, in the Add Printer Wizard, click the Add a Local Printer option (see Figure 10-1).

4. In the resulting wizard window (the Choose a Printer Port dialog box, as shown in Figure 10-2), click the down arrow on the Use an existing port field and select a port, or just use the recommended port setting that Windows selects for you. Click Next.

Figure 10-1: The Add Printer Wizard

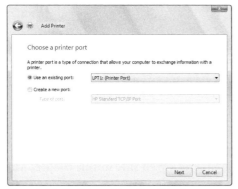

Figure 10-2: The Select a Printer Port dialog box

5. In the next wizard window (Install the Printer Driver dialog box; see Figure 10-3), choose a manufacturer and then choose a printer. You then have two options:

   • If you have the manufacturer's disc, insert it in the appropriate CD drive now and click the Have Disk button. Click Next.

   • If you don't have the manufacturer's disc, click the Windows Update button to see a list of printer drivers that you can download from Microsoft's Web site. Click Next.

6. In the resulting Type a Printer Name dialog box (see Figure 10-4), enter a printer name. If you don't want this to be your default printer, clear the Make This My Default Printer option. Click Next.

7. In the resulting dialog box, click Finish to complete the Add Printer Wizard.

 If your computer is on a network, you get an additional dialog box in the wizard right after you name the printer. Select the Do Not Share This Printer option to stop others from using the printer, or you can select the Share Name option and enter a printer name to share the printer on your network. This means that others can see and select this printer to print to.

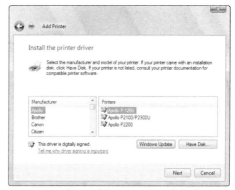

Figure 10-3: The Install the Printer Driver dialog box

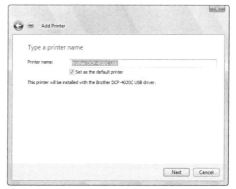

Figure 10-4: The Type a Printer Name dialog box

Set a Default Printer

1. Choose Start⇨Control Panel⇨Printer (under the Hardware and Sound category).

2. In the resulting Printers window (as shown in Figure 10-5), the current default printer is indicated by a check mark.

3. Right-click any printer that isn't set as the default and choose Set as Default Printer from the shortcut menu, as shown in Figure 10-6.

4. Click the Close button in the Printers window to save the new settings.

 To modify printing properties (for example, whether the printer prints in draft or high-quality mode, or whether it uses color or only black and white), right-click a printer in the Printers window (refer to Figure 10-6) and choose Printing Preferences. This same dialog box is available from most common Windows-based software programs, such as Microsoft Word or Excel, by clicking the Properties button in the Print dialog box.

 If you right click the printer that is already set as the default you'll find that the Set as Default Printer command will not be available on the shortcut menu mentioned in Step 3.

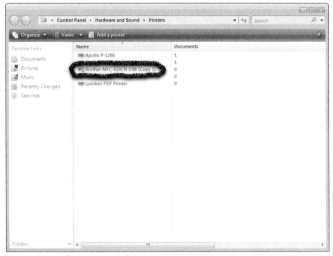

Figure 10-5: The Printers window

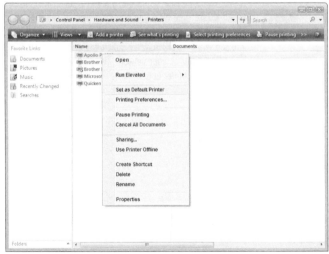

Figure 10-6: The shortcut menu to change a default printer

Configure a USB Device

1. Choose Start➪Control Panel➪Hardware and Sound➪ Device Manager.

2. In the resulting Device Manager dialog box, click the plus sign to the left of the Universal Serial Bus Controllers item. Right-click an item and choose Enable to enable it or Disable to disable it.

3. Right-click an item and choose Properties (see Figure 10-7), and then click the Drivers tab.

4. Click the Driver tab, as shown in Figure 10-8. Click the buttons on the Driver sheet to manage the driver; you can view details about it, upgrade it to a newer version, or uninstall it.

5. Click OK to save your USB device settings.

 If a USB device isn't working properly, click the Resources tab of the USB Device Properties dialog box. This includes a list of any conflicting devices that could be causing problems. Also, check the Help and Support Center for Windows (Start➪Help and Support) to locate troubleshooting help.

Figure 10-7: The General tab

Figure 10-8: The Driver tab

Set Up a Modem

1. Choose Start⇨Control Panel⇨Hardware and Sound⇨ Device Manager.

2. In the resulting Device Manager window, click the plus sign to the left of the Modems to display installed modem devices (see Figure 10-9). Right-click a modem and choose Properties from the shortcut menu.

3. In the resulting Properties dialog box, click the Modem tab, as shown in Figure 10-10. You can adjust the following settings on this tab sheet:

    *   **Speaker Volume:** Adjust the speaker volume or turn it off by using the Speaker Volume slider to control the dialing sound you hear when the modem operates.

    *   **Maximum Port Speed:** Adjust this setting by selecting a speed from the drop-down list. This setting determines the speed at which programs can send data to the modem. This is usually set at the correct number when you install the modem.

    *   **Dial Control:** Make sure that this check box is selected so your dialing attempts pay off.

4. Click the Driver tab.

     You might want to adjust modem speed if you're using a device that can support higher speeds than your installed modem. A Windows CE device is one example of this.

5. On the resulting Driver tab sheet (refer to Figure 10-8), click the buttons on the Driver sheet to manage the driver; you can view details about it, upgrade to a newer version, enable or disable it, or uninstall it.

6. Click OK to save your settings.

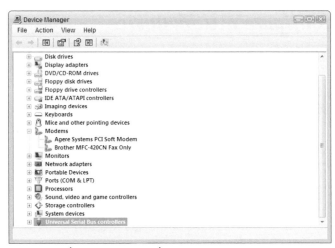

Figure 10-9: The Device Manager window

Figure 10-10: The Modem Properties dialog box

Set Up a New Monitor

1. Place the CD that came with your monitor in your CD-ROM drive and choose Start⇨Control Panel⇨ Hardware and Sound⇨Device Manager.

2. In the resulting Device Manager window, click the plus sign to the left of Monitors to display installed monitors (see Figure 10-11). Right-click the new monitor and choose Scan for Hardware Changes from the shortcut menu.

3. If your monitor driver is up to date, you see a message that scanning is in progress, which disappears when the scan is complete. If your monitor driver isn't up to date, the Hardware Update Wizard appears. Follow the wizard screens to install the monitor drivers.

4. When the wizard is complete, if everything seems to be working fine, you can close the Device Manager window.

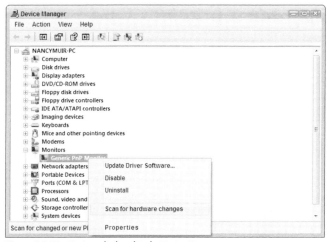

Figure 10-11: Monitors displayed in the Device Manager

 If you have problems with the monitor, open the Device Manager window, right-click the monitor, and then choose Properties. On the Driver tab, make sure the device shows a Disable button (meaning it's currently enabled). If things still aren't working right, check out Windows Help and Support for troubleshooting advice.

 Many manufacturers' device drivers are already stored in Windows. When you install a device by using the Hardware Update Wizard, you might find that you can simply browse the manufacturers' device drivers rather than download them or select them from a CD.

 You can make adjustments to your monitor display by using the Appearance and Personalization category of the Control Panel or the Display Item in Windows Classic View of Control Panel options. For more about making Display option settings, take a gander at Chapter 12.

Upgrade a Graphics Card

1. Turn off your computer. (*Note:* This step is very important; you have to open your CPU for this procedure, and you're in danger of severe electrical shock if you leave your computer on while you play around inside it.)

2. Refer to your computer manual to determine how to open the CPU, how your computer is configured, where graphics cards can be inserted, and which kinds of graphics cards to use.

3. Plug the graphics card into the appropriate slot, close your computer, and replace any screws that you took out when opening the computer.

4. Turn on the computer; Windows Vista detects the new card and installs appropriate drivers.

5. View the information about the installed graphics device by choosing Start➪Control Panel➪Hardware and Sound➪Device Manager.

6. Click the plus sign next to Display Adapters (see Figure 10-12), right-click the graphics card that you installed, and then choose Properties. You see system settings for this card (see Figure 10-13). The Device Status tells you whether it's working properly.

 Note that your particular hardware might have its own idiosyncrasies, and new technologies come along that change the way newer computers are configured, so be sure to read your computer users' manual before dealing with any hardware upgrade.

 Warning: Be careful about poking metal implements (such as screwdrivers) into the insides of the CPU because you could set off an electrical unpleasantry. Place your computer on a nonconductive surface (such as a rubber mat) before opening it up. Don't wear an aluminum foil suit for this sort of procedure, and *never* leave your computer plugged in or turned on while opening it.

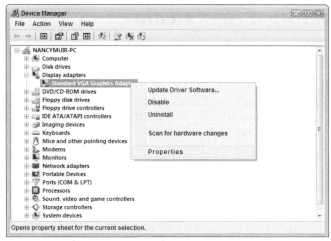

Figure 10-12: The Device Manager window

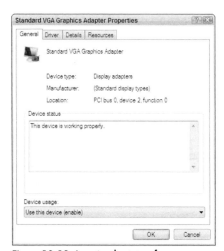

Figure 10-13: Assessing the status of your new graphics card

Set Up a Sound Card

1. Choose Start⇨Control Panel⇨Hardware and Sound, and then click the Device Manager link.

2. In the resulting Device Manager window (see Figure 10-14), click the plus sign icon to the left of Sound, Video, and Game Controllers.

3. Right-click the sound card listed there and choose Properties.

4. In the resulting Audio Controller Properties dialog box shown in Figure 10-15, on the Driver tab, make sure the fourth button down says Disable (meaning the device is currently enabled). If it says Enable, click on it.

5. If you want to make changes to the driver, click the Update Driver button.

6. When you're done making settings, click OK.

 Read your users' manual before doing this procedure. Some sound cards are built into the motherboard, but others require that you take some steps to disable the old card before installing the new.

 If you're having trouble getting sound, remember the basics: You have to have speakers connected to your computer, and the volume setting on your computer can't be muted. If you neglect to properly set either of these two vital requirements, don't be ashamed — just about everyone has done it, myself included!

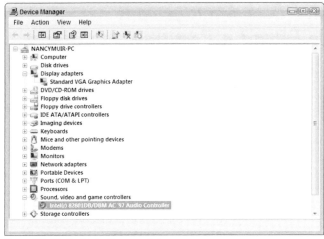

Figure 10-14: The Device Manager window

Figure 10-15: The Audio Controller Properties dialog box, General tab

Use Disk Management to Extend a Partition

1. Choose Start⇨Control Panel⇨System and Maintenance⇨ Administrative Tools.

2. In the resulting Administrative Tools windows, double-click Computer Management.

3. In the resulting Computer Management window (as shown in Figure 10-16), click Disk Management in the list on the left (the Disk Management window shown in Figure 10-17 appears), right-click a basic disk in the top center pane (this is usually your hard drive) that isn't allocated, and then choose Extend Volume from the shortcut menu that appears.

4. Follow the steps in the New Simple Volume Wizard to create the new partition.

 An extended partition adds to your drive space by borrowing some from an adjoining partition, and makes your system utilize memory more efficiently. But just so you know, you have to be logged on as a system administrator to complete the steps listed here.

 You can also shrink a drive, which frees up some space for you to create a new partition at the end of a volume. The Shrink Volume command is located on the shortcut menu that appears when you right-click a disk in the Disk Management window.

Figure 10-16: The Computer Management window

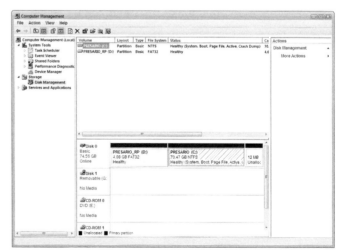

Figure 10-17: The Disk Management window

Setting Up a Network

Chapter 11

Get ready to . . .

Setting up a network among two or more computers can make your life much easier because after you set up a network, you can use this connection to share files, folders, printers, and access to the Internet with other users.

The most common way to connect a network is to use a wired Ethernet connection, involving cables and equipment, referred to as a *hub* or *switch*. To determine whether your computer is Ethernet-ready, check the back of your PC: You should see what looks like a very large phone connector jack. This is the Ethernet connector.

After you connect the necessary cables and equipment, most newer computers already have network drivers installed, so Windows Vista is capable of recognizing the connection. With simple-to-use wizards, little input on your part is required to set up a network.

You can also set up a connection through a wireless access point (which you set up according to the instructions that come with the wireless router) and an adapter that you either install in your CPU in the form of a PCI adapter or plug into your PC by using a USB (Universal Serial Bus) port or a PC Card adapter.

To set up a network, you explore the following tasks:

- Installing a network adapter if one is not built into your computer, and configuring a network by using the Network Setup Wizard.
- Setting up a wireless access point and configuring a wireless network by using the Wireless Network Setup Wizard.
- Making various settings to a network connection, including changing a networked computer's name so the one you gave it when you bought it (Hot Mama, Road Warrior, or whatever) isn't the one that shows on the network.
- Creating and viewing workgroups on a network.

Install a PCI Network Adapter

1. After purchasing the PCI adapter, turn off your desktop computer and disconnect all power and other cables from it.

2. Open the PC chassis (see Figure 11-1). Check your user's manual for this procedure, which usually involves removing a few screws and popping the cover off your tower.

3. Touch a metal object (not the computer) to get rid of any static discharge before you reach inside the computer.

4. Locate an empty slot for the PCI adapter and if necessary remove the protective cover from it. Again, check your manual for the exact location in your system.

5. Remove the adapter from its packaging. Handling it by its edges, line it up with the slot and insert it firmly but gently.

6. Make sure you don't disconnect any wires or leave loose screws inside the PC chassis; then replace the computer cover and reinsert the screws.

 Leave the parts that you're going to insert in your computer in their packaging until you need them. If they sit around on your desktop or elsewhere, they could pick up static discharge, which could be harmful to your computer.

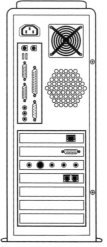

Figure 11-1: Opening your CPU case

7. Plug in the computer and turn it on. Your computer should sense the new adapter when it starts up and display the Installing Device Driver pop-up above your taskbar (see Figure 11-2).

8. Windows Vista might automatically set up the hardware. If Windows Vista can't find a driver for the adapter, you might have to provide it.

9. When the process is complete, a pop-up appears stating that your hardware driver is installed and ready to use (see Figure 11-3).

 If Windows Vista cannot find the driver, use the diskette or CD that came with the adapter — or you can usually download the driver from your hardware manufacturer's Web site for free. Use the Browse button to navigate to the location where you downloaded the driver, and then proceed with the wizard.

Figure 11-2: The Installing Device Driver pop-up

Figure 11-3: Confirmation that your device driver was installed

Connect a Wired Ethernet Network

1. Obtain a Cat 5 or Cat 5e Ethernet cable for every computer you will connect to the network (see Figure 11-4).

2. Purchase a hub or switch with enough ports for each computer you want to connect (see Figure 11-5).

3. Turn off all computers as well as the switch/hub. Plug one end of the Ethernet cable into the switch or hub and the other end into the network adapter that you installed in your PC. See the first task in this chapter for help with this.

4. Repeat Step 3 for each computer you want to include in the network.

5. Turn on the switch or hub and then turn on the computers. Use the following task to run the Network Setup Wizard and set up the network.

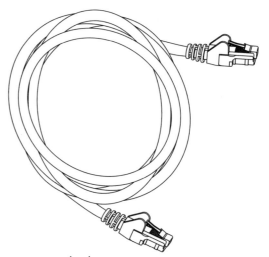

Figure 11-4: The Ethernet connector

 Switches make for a speedier network although they cost a little more than a hub. However, in most cases, it's better to invest a few dollars more for the extra performance of a switch. If you want to get very sophisticated — for example, like on a company network — you could use a router, which helps you track various people on the network and the places they are going on the network.

 Cat 5 is a kind of cable used for data transfer. If your home is wired for high-speed access, you may have Cat 5 cable in your walls. You can find the kind of Cat 5 cable referred to in this task at your local computer or office supply store with connectors for plugging into your comptuer and hub.

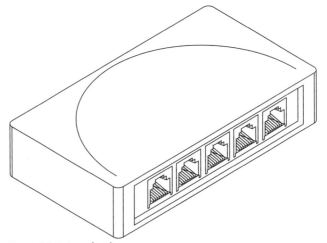

Figure 11-5: A switch with ports

Configure a Wireless Network by Using the Network Setup Wizard

1. Turn on each PC that you have attached to the network.

2. On the PC that will share its Internet connection, log on to the Internet.

3. On the Internet-connection PC, choose Start⇨Network and then click the Network and Sharing Center button.

4. In the resulting Network and Sharing Center window, click the Set Up a Connection or Network link.

5. In the resulting Choose a Connection Option window (see Figure 11-6), choose the Set Up a Wireless Network option and then click Next. The next window describes what the wizard will do; click Next.

6. A progress windows displays (see Figure 11-7) while Windows Vista detects your hardware settings. There are a few options at this point:

   • Windows Vista detects your hardware and configures it automatically; you are done.

   • Windows Vista detects your hardware but requires you to configure it manually. In this case, select the Configure This Device Manually option and complete the required information to finish the setup.

   • If you have a Flash drive connected via a USB port, connect the drive and click the Create Wireless Network Settings and Save to a USB Flash Drive. Enter a name for your network on the following screen and then follow the directions, which involve disconnecting the Flash drive and plugging it into a wireless access point. You can then use the drive to configure each computer on the network as directed.

7. On the final wizard screen that appears, click Finish.

 When you purchase a wireless access point, it includes instructions for setting it up. This typically involves plugging it into a power source, plugging in Ethernet cables to your main computer and possibly a DSL (digital subscriber line) or other high-speed modem, and then turning it on.

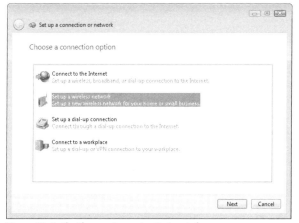

Figure 11-6: The Choose a Connection Option window

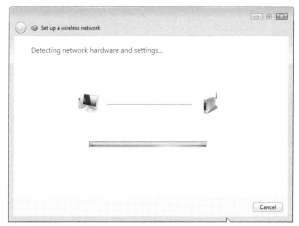

Figure 11-7: Choosing how to set up your network

123

Change a Computer's Network Name

1. Choose Start↭Control Panel↭System and Maintenance and then click the System link.

2. In the resulting System dialog box, as shown in Figure 11-8, click the Change Settings link.

3. On the Computer Name tab of the resulting System Properties dialog box, as shown in Figure 11-9, replace the current name with a name in the Computer Description text box and then click OK to save the new name.

4. Click the Close button to close the Control Panel.

 Two computers on the same network cannot have the same name. Therefore, you may want to modify computer names before you start setting up your network so they are unique. Making the computer name descriptive is useful: Simple names such as *John's Computer* and *Basement PC* help everybody on the network know which is which.

Figure 11-8: The System window of the Control Panel

Figure 11-9: The System Properties dialog box, Computer Name tab

Join a Workgroup

1. Choose Start⇨Control Panel⇨System and Maintenance and then click the System link.

2. In the resulting System dialog box, click the Change Settings link.

3. On the Computer Name tab of the resulting System Properties dialog box, shown in Figure 11-10, click the Change button.

4. The Computer Name/Domain Changes dialog box appears (see Figure 11-11). In the Workgroup field, enter or edit the name for your workgroup *with no spaces between letters.*

5. Click OK to close the dialog box, and then click OK again to close the System Properties dialog box. If prompted, restart Windows Vista.

 A *workgroup* is essentially a set of computers on a network. On a large network, breaking computers down into these groups so they can easily work with each other makes sense. In a smaller home network, you will probably just create one workgroup to allow all your computers to easily access each other.

 One task that becomes easier when you are part of a workgroup is sharing files. If you locate a file or folder on your computer and right-click it, you can choose to share it on the network. When you do, only people in your workgroup will be able to access this shared file or folder.

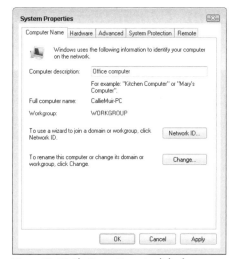

Figure 11-10: The System Properties dialog box, Computer Name tab

Figure 11-11: The Computer Name/ Domain Changes dialog box

View Workgroup Computers

1. Choose Start➪Network.

2. In the resulting window, click the Network and Sharing Center button. In the Network and Sharing Center window, click the View Computers and Devices link.

3. In the resulting window, click the arrow on the Views button, as shown in Figure 11-12, and choose Details. The Workgroup column lists the names of all network workgroups.

4. Click the Close button to close the window.

 When you view a workgroup, you can double-click one to see a listing of all the devices, scheduled tasks, and shared files and folders available to the group.

 If you don't see a computer you expected to see on your network, double-check to see if you entered the workgroup name correctly in the preceding task of Joining a Workgroup. Workgroups can have no spaces, and all computers in the workgroup have to have exactly the same workgroup name—no typos!

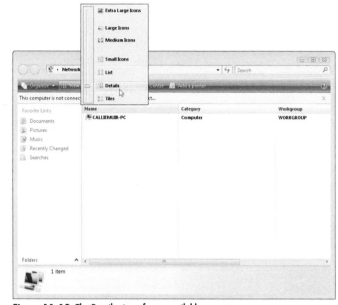

Figure 11-12: The Details view of your available computers

Part IV

Customizing the Windows Desktop

The 5th Wave   By Rich Tennant

"How do you like that Aero glass interface on Vista? Nice, huh?"

Setting Up Your Display

You chose your designer Day Planner, glow-in-the-dark gel pens, and solid maple inbox for your real-world desktop, right? Why shouldn't the Windows Vista desktop give you the same flexibility to make things look the way you like? After all, this is the main work area of Windows Vista, a space that you traverse many, many times in a typical workday. Take it from somebody who spends many hours in front of a computer: Customizing your desktop pays off in increased productivity as well as decreased eyestrain.

To customize your desktop, you can do the following:

➡ **Change how the desktop looks**. Set up Windows Vista to display images and colors. You can also use screen saver settings to switch from everyday work stuff to a pretty animation when you've stopped working for a time. You can modify your *screen resolution* setting, which controls how sharp and detailed a picture your screen displays.

➡ **Rearrange icons.** Your desktop isn't just a pretty picture. Placed on the background are icons that represent shortcuts to the programs and files that you work with every day. Organizing these icons logically can help you be more efficient.

Set Your Screen's Resolution

1. Right-click the desktop to display a shortcut menu and then choose Personalize.

2. In the resulting Personalization window, click the Display Settings link.

3. In the Display Settings dialog box that appears (as shown in Figure 12-1), move the Resolution slider to a higher or lower resolution. You can also choose how many colors your computer uses for display by making a choice in the Colors drop-down list.

4. Click OK to accept the new screen resolution.

Figure 12-1: The Display Settings dialog box

 Higher resolutions, such as 1400 x 1250, produce smaller, crisper images. Lower resolutions, such as 800 x 600, produce larger, somewhat jagged images. The upside of higher resolution is that more fits on your screen; the downside is that words and graphics can be hard to see.

 The Colors setting of the Display Properties dialog box offers two settings. The lower color quality is 16-bit; the highest is 32-bit. Essentially, the higher the bits, the more color definition you get.

 Remember that you can also use your View settings in most software programs to get a larger or smaller view of your documents without having to change your screen's resolution.

Change the Desktop Background

1. Right-click the desktop and choose Personalize from the shortcut menu.

2. In the resulting Personalization window, click the Desktop Background link to display the Desktop Background dialog box, as shown in Figure 12-2.

3. Select a category of desktop background options from the Background list box (see Figure 12-3) and then click the image preview you want to use. The background is previewed on your desktop.

4. From the positioning options at the bottom, select one of the following options:

   • **Fit to Screen:** This option stretches one copy of the image to fill the screen, covering any background color completely.

   • **Tile:** This choice displays multiple copies of the image filling the desktop. The number of images depends on the size and resolution of the original graphic.

   • **Center:** Quite logically, this option centers the image on a colored background so that you can see a border of color around its edges.

5. Click OK to apply the settings and close the dialog box.

 If you apply a desktop theme (see more about this in the next task), you overwrite whatever desktop settings you've made in this task. If you apply a desktop theme and then go back and make desktop settings, you replace the theme's settings. However, making changes is easy and keeps your desktop interesting, so play around with themes and desktop backgrounds all you like!

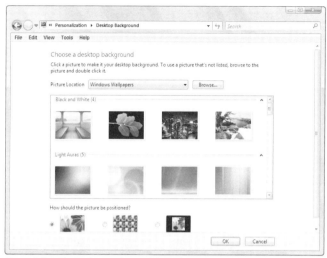

Figure 12-2: The Desktop Background dialog box

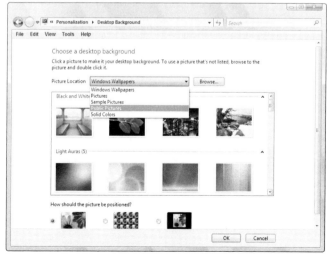

Figure 12-3: Available categories of backgrounds

Choose a Desktop Theme

1. Right-click the desktop and choose Personalize. The Personalization window opens. Click the Theme link.

2. In the resulting Theme Settings dialog box, as shown in Figure 12-4, select a theme from the Theme drop-down list. Your options include the following:

   • **Windows Vista** offers up a beautiful lake and mountains against a blue sky. The color scheme that this theme uses for various onscreen elements, such as window title bars, relies heavily on grays, blues, and reds.

   • **Windows Classic** sports a plain blue background with silvery-blue and gray colors for screen elements.

   • **My Current Theme** uses whatever settings you have and saves them with that name.

   • **Browse** takes you to the Program Files folder of Windows, where you can look for any files with the `.theme` extension. It's not that Windows Vista comes with a lot of these waiting in this folder for you to use them, but if you buy and install Microsoft Plus! which provides you with lots of extra graphic goodies, the new themes are stored here by default. If you find one you like, select, and click the Open button.

3. Click OK to apply the selected theme.

 Themes save sets of elements that include menu appearance, background colors or patterns, screen savers, and even mouse cursors and sounds. If you modify any of these individually — for example, by changing the screen saver to another one — that change overrides the setting in the theme you last applied.

Figure 12-4: The Theme Settings dialog box

 You can save custom themes. Simply apply a theme, make any changes to it you like using the various Appearance and Personalization settings options, and then in the Theme Settings dialog box, click Save As. In the resulting dialog box give your new theme a name and click Save. It will now appear on the Theme list.

Set Up a Screen Saver

1. Right-click the desktop and choose Personalize. In the resulting Personalization window, click the Screen Saver link to display the Screen Saver Settings dialog box, as shown in Figure 12-5.

2. From the Screen Saver drop-down list, choose a screen saver.

3. Use the arrows in the Wait *xx* Minutes text box to set the number of inactivity minutes that Windows Vista waits before displaying the screen saver.

4. Click the Preview button (see Figure 12-6) to take a peek at your screen saver of choice. When you're happy with your settings, click OK.

Figure 12-5: The Screen Saver Settings dialog box

 Screen savers used to be required to keep your monitor from burning out because an image was held on your screen for too long. Newer monitors don't require this, but people are attached to their screen savers, so the feature persists. Screen savers are also useful for hiding what's on your screen from curious passersby if you happen to wander away from your desk for a while. If you want no screen saver to appear, choose None from the Screen Saver list in the Screen Saver Settings dialog box.

 Some screen savers allow you to modify their settings: for example, how fast they display or how many lines they draw onscreen. To customize this, click the Settings button when in the Screen Saver Settings dialog box.

Figure 12-6: The Aquarium screen saver preview

Change the Windows Vista Color Scheme

1. Right-click the desktop and choose Personalize.

2. In the resulting Personalization window, click the Window Color and Appearance link to display the Appearance Settings dialog box, as shown in Figure 12-7.

3. Click a color scheme and make settings for transparency and color intensity.

4. To customize the selected preset color scheme, click the Open Classic Appearance Properties for More Color Options link, and in the Appearance settings dialog box that appears, click Advanced.

5. In the resulting Advanced Appearance dialog box, as shown in Figure 12-8, click a screen element in the Item drop down list and then make settings for size, color, font, or effects such as bold and repeat this for each item you want to change.

6. Click OK to close the Advanced Appearance dialog box and apply all changes.

 If you want to set specific colors in the Advanced Appearance dialog box and you know the Red/Green/Blue value for those colors, in the Color drop down lists click Other and enter specific values for Red, Green, and Blue. Click OK to save the changes.

 Some colors are easier on the eyes than others. For example, green is more restful to look at than orange. Choose a color scheme that is pleasant to look at and easy on the eyes!

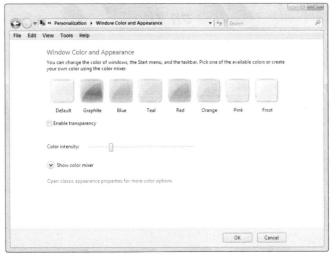

Figure 12-7: The Appearance Settings dialog box

Figure 12-8: The Advanced Appearance dialog box

Arrange Icons on the Desktop

1. Modify the icons displayed on your desktop by using any of these methods:

- Right-click the Windows desktop. In the resulting shortcut menu (as shown in Figure 12-9), choose Sort By, and then choose one of four criteria: Name, Size, File Extension, or Date Modified.

- Click any icon on the desktop and drag it to a new location.

- Right-click the Windows desktop, choose View, and then make sure that Auto Arrange isn't selected. (If it is selected, deselect it.) Now you can click any icon and drag it to another location on the desktop.

2. To automatically add certain folders to your desktop, right-click the desktop and choose Personalize. In the resulting Personalization window, click the Change Desktop Icons link in the Task pane.

3. In the resulting Desktop Icon Settings dialog box, as shown in Figure 12-10, select any of the Desktop Icons check boxes to automatically display shortcuts for items such as Internet Explorer, the Computer, or the Recycle Bin.

4. Click OK to save the settings and click Close to close the Personalization window.

Figure 12-9: The desktop shortcut menu

Figure 12-10: The Desktop Icon Settings dialog box

To change an icon used for the preset folders that you set up in the Desktop Icon Settings dialog box, select an icon preview and click the Change Icon button. In the Change Icon dialog box that appears, click another icon, and then click OK twice. However, be careful when using this feature: If somebody who uses your computer isn't aware of the changed icons, he could start clicking the wrong icon and potentially not only waste time but possibly run a program that you don't want him to run. If you make changes and decide to go back to Microsoft's original idea of a good icon for programs, click the Restore Default button in the Desktop Icon Settings dialog box.

Customizing Windows Ease of Access

*P*eople aren't born with good manners. Everyone has to be taught to help other people and share toys, for example. Similarly, sometimes Windows has to be taught how to behave. For example, it doesn't know right off the bat that somebody using it has a vision challenge that requires special help, or that a user prefers a certain mouse cursor, or that you have difficulty using your keyboard.

Somebody taught you manners, but Windows depends on you to make settings that customize its behavior. This is good news for you because the ability to customize Windows Vista gives you a lot of flexibility in how you interact with it.

Here's what you can do to customize Windows Vista:

➡ Control features that help visually challenged users to work with a computer, such as setting a higher contrast or using a Narrator to read the onscreen text aloud.

➡ Work with the Speech Recognition feature that allows you to input data into a document using speech rather than a keyboard or mouse.

➡ Modify the mouse functionality for left-handed use, change the cursor to sport a certain look, or make viewing the cursor as it moves around your screen easier.

➡ Work with keyboard settings that make input easier for those who are challenged by physical conditions, such as carpal tunnel syndrome or arthritis.

Optimize the Visual Display

1. Choose Start➪Control Panel.

2. In the Control Panel window, click the Optimize Visual Display link under the Ease of Access tools.

3. In the resulting Optimize Visual Display dialog box (as shown in Figure 13-1), select the check boxes for features you want to use:

- **High Contrast:** Make settings for using greater contrast on screen elements.

- **Make Things on the Screen Larger:** If you click Turn on Magnifier (see Figure 13-2), you have two cursors onscreen. One cursor appears in the Magnifier window where everything is shown enlarged, and one appears in whatever is showing on your computer (for example, your desktop or an open application). You can maneuver either cursor to work in your document. (They're both active, so it does take some getting used to.)

- **Make Things On Screen Easier to See:** Here's where you make settings that adjust onscreen contrast to make things easier to see, enlarge the size of the blinking mouse cursor, and get rid of distracting animations and backgrounds.

4. When you finish making settings, click Save to apply them.

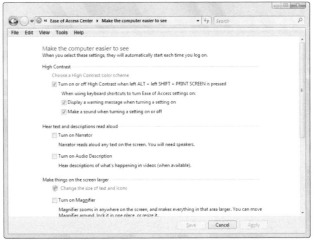

Figure 13-1: Magnifying your text

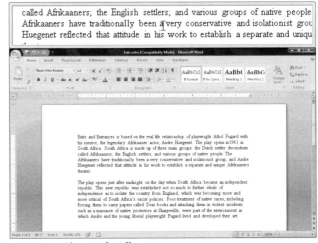

Figure 13-2: The Magnifier effect on your screen

Replace Sounds with Visual Cues

1. Choose Start⇨Control Panel⇨Ease of Access and then click the Replace Sounds with Visual Cues link.

2. In the resulting Sounds dialog box (see Figure 13-3), make any of the following settings:

- Turn on Visual Notifications so that Windows Vista will play sounds along with a display of visual cues.

- Chose a setting for visual warnings. These warnings essentially flash a portion of your screen to alert you to an event.

- To control text captions for any spoken words, select Turn on Text Captions for Spoken Dialog (when available). *Note:* This isn't always available with every application you use.

3. To save the new settings, click Save.

 Visual cues are useful if you are hard of hearing and don't always pick up system sounds alerting you to error messages or a device disconnect. After the setting is turned on, it is active until you go back to the Sounds dialog box and turn it off.

 This may seem obvious, but if you are hard of hearing you may want to simply increase the volume for your speakers. You can do this by using the volume adjustment in a program such as Windows Media Player (see Chapter 21), or modifying your system volume by choosing Hardware and Sound in the Control Panel and then clicking the Adjust System Volume link.

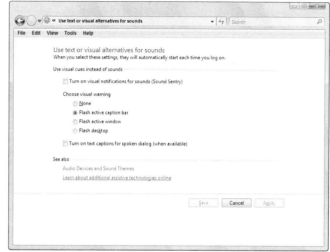

Figure 13-3: The Sounds dialog box

Set Up Speech Recognition

1. Attach a desktop microphone or headset to your computer and choose Start⇨Control Panel⇨Ease of Access⇨ Start Speech Recognition.

2. The Set Up Speech Recognition message appears; click Next to continue. (*Note:* If you've used Speech Recognition before, this message will not appear.)

3. In the resulting Welcome to Speech Recognition dialog box (as shown in Figure 13-4), select the type of microphone that you're using and then click Next. The next screen tells you how to place and use the microphone for optimum results. Click Next.

4. In the following window (see Figure 13-5), read the sample sentence aloud. When you're done, click Next.

During the Speech Recognition setup procedure you are given the option of printing out commonly used commands. It's a good idea to do this, as speech commands aren't always second nature!

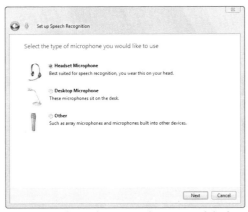

Figure 13-4: The initial Set Up Speech Recognition dialog box

Figure 13-5: The dialog box where you establish your microphone connection by reading a sentence aloud

5. In the resulting dialog box, choose whether to enable or disable document view. Document view allows Windows Vista to review your documents and e-mail to help it recognize your speech patterns. Click Next.

6. In the resulting dialog box, if you wish to view and/or print a list of speech recognition commands, click the View Reference Sheet button, and then click the Close button to close that window. Click Next to proceed.

7. In the resulting dialog box, either click Run Speech Recognition at Startup to disable this feature or leave the default setting. Click Next. The final dialog box informs you that you can now control the computer by voice, and offers you a Start Tutorial button to help you practice voice commands. Click that button, or click Cancel to skip the tutorial and leave the Speech Recognition set up.

8. The Speech Recognition control panel appears (see Figure 13-6). Say, "Start listening" to activate the feature and begin using spoken commands to work with your computer.

Figure 13-6: The Speech Recognition Control Panel

To stop Speech Recognition, click the Close button on the Control Panel. To start the Speech Recognition feature again, choose Start➪Control Panel➪Ease of Access➪Speech Recognition and then click the Start Speech Recognition link. To learn more about Speech Recognition commands, click the Take Speech Tutorials link in the Ease of Access window.

Modify How Your Keyboard Works

1. Choose Start⇨Control Panel⇨Ease of Access and then click the Change How Your Keyboard Works link.

2. In the resulting Keyboard dialog box (see Figure 13-7), make any of these settings:

   • Turn on Mouse Keys to control your mouse by keyboard commands. If you turn on this setting, click the Set Up Mouse Keys link to specify settings for this feature.

   • Select the Turn on Sticky Keys feature to set up keystroke combinations to be pressed one at a time, rather than in combination.

   • You can set up Windows Vista to play a sound when you press Caps Lock, Num Lock, or Scroll Lock (which I do all the time by mistake!).

   • If you sometimes press a key very lightly or press it so hard it activates twice, you can use the Turn on Filter Keys setting to adjust repeat rates to adjust for that. Use the Set Up Filter Keys link to fine-tune settings if you make this choice.

   • To have Windows Vista highlight keyboard shortcuts and access keys with an underline wherever these shortcuts appear, click that setting.

3. To save the new settings, click Save.

 You can click the Learn about Additional Assistive Technologies Online link to go the Microsoft Web site and discover add-on and third-party programs that might help you if you have a visual, hearing, or input-related disability.

Figure 13-7: The Keyboard dialog box

 Keyboards all have their own unique feel. If your keyboard isn't responsive and you have a keyboard-challenging condition, you might also try different keyboards to see if one works better for you than another.

Use the Onscreen Keyboard Feature

1. Choose Start⇨Control Panel⇨Ease of Access and then click the Ease of Access Center link.

2. In the resulting Change Ease of Access Center dialog box (see Figure 13-8), select the Start On-Screen Keyboard check box. The On-Screen Keyboard appears.

3. Open a document in any application where you can enter text, and then click the keys on the onscreen keyboard to make entries.

 To use keystroke combinations (such as Ctrl+Z), click first key (in this case, Ctrl), and then click the second key (Z). You don't have to hold down the first key as you do with a regular keyboard.

4. To change settings, such as how you select keys (Typing Mode) or the font used to label keys (Font), choose Settings and then choose one of the four options shown in Figure 13-9.

5. Click the Close button to stop using the onscreen keyboard.

 You can set up the Hover typing mode to activate a key after you hover your mouse over it for a predefined period of time (x number of seconds). If you have arthritis or some other condition that makes clicking your mouse difficult, this option can help you enter text. Choose Settings⇨Typing Mode⇨Hover to Select to activate the Hover mode.

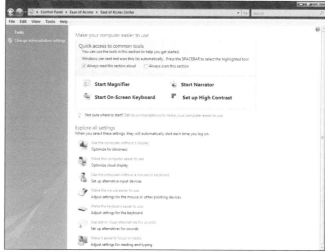

Figure 13-8: The Change Ease of Access window

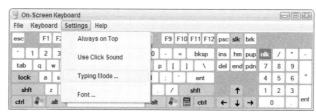

Figure 13-9: The On-Screen Keyboard Settings menu

Change Mouse Behavior

1. Choose Start⇨Control Panel⇨Ease of Access and then click the Change How Your Mouse Works link. The Make the Mouse Easier to Use dialog box opens (see Figure 13-10).

2. To use the numeric keypad to move your mouse cursor on your screen, choose the Turn on Mouse Keys setting. If you turn this feature on, click Set Up Mouse Keys to fine-tune its behavior.

3. Select the Activate a Window by Hovering Over It with The Mouse check box to enable this (pretty self-explanatory!) feature.

4. Click Save to save the new settings.

 You can click the Mouse Settings link in the Mouse Properties dialog box; then, on the Buttons tab, use the Switch Primary and Secondary Buttons feature to make the right mouse button handle all the usual left button functions, such as clicking and dragging, and the left button handle the typical right-hand functions, such as displaying shortcut menus. This helps left-handed people use the mouse more easily.

 If you want to modify the behavior of the mouse pointer, in the Mouse Properties dialog box, click the Pointer Options tab to set the pointer speed (how quickly you can drag the mouse pointer around your screen), to activate the Snap To feature that automatically moves the mouse cursor to the default choice in a dialog box, or to modify the little trails that appear when you drag the pointer.

 If you have difficulty seeing the cursor on-screen experiment with the Windows Vista color scheme to see if another setting makes your cursor stand out better against the background. See Chapter 12 for information on setting up the color scheme for your computer.

Figure 13-10: The Make the Mouse Easier to Use dialog box

Change the Cursor

1. Choose Start⇨Control Panel⇨Ease of Access⇨Change How Your Mouse Works.

2. Click any mouse pointer sample to select it (see Figure 13-11).

3. Click Apply to use the new pointer setting and then click Save to close the Mouse dialog box.

 Be careful not to change the cursor to another standard cursor (for example, changing the Normal Select cursor to the Busy hourglass cursor). This could prove slightly confusing for you and completely baffling to anybody else who works on your computer. If you make a choice and decide it was a mistake, click the Use Default button on Pointer tab in the Mouse Properties dialog box to return a selected cursor to its default choice.

 To change other cursors, for example the cursor that appears when you click and drag objects, click the Mouse Settings link, Pointers tab.

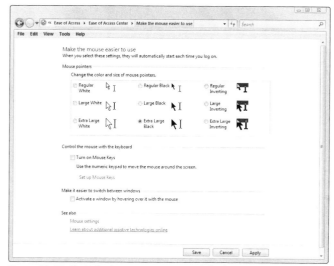

Figure 13-11: The Make the Mouse Easier to Use dialog box

Part V
Using Security and Maintenance Features

The 5th Wave   By Rich Tennant

"Well, the first level of Windows Vista security seems good—I can't get the shrink-wrapping off."

Setting Passwords and File Access

*A*fter working with Windows and the software that it supports for a while, you'll find that you build a treasure trove of information and documents. Microsoft provides features in Windows that help to keep your computer private, whether at work or home, as well as to protect your valuable files. These features include the following:

➟ With passwords assigned (password-protection), you can keep people from accessing your computer when you're not around.

➟ Shared and public folder features allow you to share information with others on a network or to keep others out of folders, if you prefer. You can also use the shared folders feature to share folders with multiple users of a standalone computer.

➟ Use settings to protect individual files by making them *read-only* — that is, allowing people to read what's in them but not make and save changes — or hidden from others entirely.

➟ Set up user accounts so that different users on a single computer access their own settings. Also, use parental controls so folks with more experience can guide those who are younger as they explore what the computer and Internet have to offer.

Chapter

14

Get ready to . . .

Change the Windows Password

1. Choose Start⇨Control Panel, and then click User Accounts and Family Safety.

2. In the resulting window shown in Figure 14-1, click the Change Your Windows Password link. Then, if you have more than one user account, click Manage Another Account and click the account to add the password to. Click the Create a Password for Your Account link.

3. In the Create a Password for Your Account screen, as shown in Figure 14-2, enter a password, confirm it, and add a password hint.

4. Click the Change Password button.

5. You return to the Make Changes to Your User Account window. If you wish to remove your password at some point, you can click the Remove Your Password link here.

6. Click the Close button to close the User Accounts window.

 If you forget your password, Windows shows the hint you entered to help you remember it, but remember that anybody who uses your computer can see the hint when it's displayed. So, if lots of people know that you drive a Ford and your hint is "My car model," your password protection is about as effective as a thin raincoat in a hurricane.

 After you create a password, you can go to the User Accounts window and change it at any time by clicking Change Your Password. You can also change the name on your user account by typing Change Your Name.

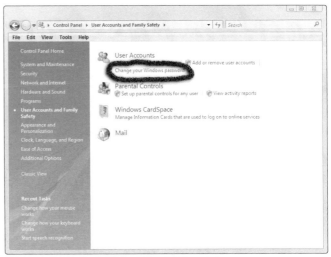

Figure 14-1: The User Accounts and Family Safety window

Figure 14-2: The Create a Password for Your Account screen

Allow Access to the Public Folder

1. Choose Start⇨Control Panel and then click the Set Up File Sharing link under the Network and Internet category.

2. In the resulting Network and Sharing dialog box (see Figure 14-3), click the arrow on the Public Sharing item and select your preferred setting for the Public Folder. You can allow access with the ability to make changes, allow access without the ability to make changes, or not allow access.

3. Click Apply to save the setting and then click the Close button to close the Control Panel.

     The Public folder is found using the path `C:\Users\Public`. This is a handy way to share files when you have protected your private folders.

     In the Network and Sharing Center dialog box, click the Show Me All the Files and Folders I Am Sharing link to review the accesses you have set up.

     Even if you allow access to a printer through printer sharing, you may need to install that printer's drivers in each computer that accesses it. See Chapter 10 for more about setting up printers.

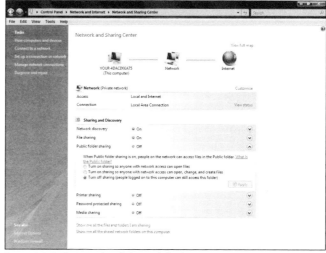

Figure 14-3: The Network and Sharing dialog box

Set Up Shared Folders

1. Locate the folder that you want to share by using Windows Explorer. (Choose Start➪All Programs➪ Accessories➪Windows Explorer.)

2. Right-click the folder that you want to allow others to access and then choose Share.

3. In the resulting File Sharing dialog box, as shown in Figure 14-4, click the arrow in the box to select users to share with, and then click Add. To create a new user, choose Create a New User from the drop-down list that appears.

4. Click Share. A dialog box appears. Click Yes to share the file. A confirmation dialog box appears indicating that the file is shared and allowing you to e-mail a link to it to the people to whom you have granted access (see Figure 14-5).

5. Click Done to complete the file sharing process.

 To find out more about using Windows Explorer to locate and work with files, see Chapter 2.

 You can choose to share individual files by following the procedure outlined here, but if you change your mind you can also remove permissions. To change the permissions for sharing a file with a particular user, display the File Sharing dialog box, click the name of a user, and choose Remove from the menu that appears.

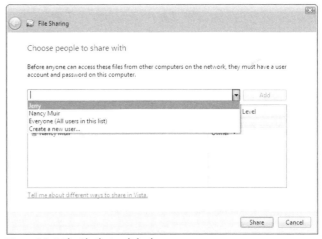

Figure 14-4: The File Sharing dialog box

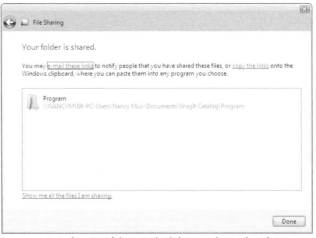

Figure 14-5: Confirmation of sharing with a link to e-mail users about their permissions

Set File Attributes

1. Locate the file that you want to modify by using Windows Explorer. (Choose Start⇨All Programs⇨ Accessories⇨Windows Explorer.)

2. Right-click the file and choose Properties.

3. In the resulting *Filename* Properties dialog box, as shown in Figure 14-6, click the General tab.

4. Select the Read-Only or Hidden check boxes.

5. Click OK to accept the new settings.

 If you want to see the files that you've marked as hidden, go to the file or folder location (for example, in the My Documents folder or by using Windows Explorer) and choose Organize⇨Folder and Search Options. Click the View tab to display it, select the Show Hidden Files and Folders radio button in the Advanced Settings, and then click OK. Be aware that this reveals all hidden folders, not just those for a particular folder.

 One other item you can change settings for in the Properties dialog box is what program you open the file with. In the Opens With area of the dialog box click the Change button and choose the most appropriate program. This is handy for items such as graphics files where you may have a preferred graphics viewing program you like to use.

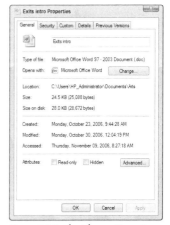

Figure 14-6: The *Filename* Properties dialog box

Create a New User Account

1. Choose Start➪Control Panel.

2. In the resulting window, click the Add or Remove User Accounts link under User Accounts and Family Safety.

3. In the resulting Manage Accounts dialog box, as shown in Figure 14-7, click Create a New Account.

4. In the next dialog box, as shown in Figure 14-8, enter an account name, and then select the type of account you want to create:

   • **Administrator,** who can do things like create and change accounts and install programs.

   • **Standard user,** who can't do the tasks an administrator can.

5. Click the Create Account button and then close the Control Panel.

 After you create an account, you can make changes to it, such as assigning a password or changing the account type, by double-clicking it in the Manage Accounts window you reached in Step 4 (in the preceding step list) and following the links listed there.

Figure 14-7: Creating a new user account

Figure 14-8: Choosing the account type

Switch User Accounts

1. Click Start and then click the arrow on the side of the Lock button (see Figure 14-9).

2. Choose Switch User. In the resulting window, click on the user you want to log in as.

3. If the user account is password-protected, a box appears for you to enter the password. Type the password and then click the arrow button to log in.

4. Windows Vista logs you in with the specified user's settings.

 If you don't like the picture associated with your user account, you can change it. Choose Start➪Control Panel➪Add or Remove User Accounts and then click the account you want to change. In the resulting window, click Change the Picture and choose another picture or browse to see more picture choices.

 If you forget your password and try to switch users without entering one, Windows Vista shows your password hint, which you can create when you assign a password to help you remember it.

 You can set up several user accounts for your computer, which helps you save and access specific user settings and provide privacy for each user's files with passwords. To find out about setting up user accounts and changing their settings, see Chapter 14.

Figure 14-9: Switching users

Set Up Parental Controls

1. Choose Start➪Control Panel➪Set Up Parental Controls For Any User under the User Accounts and Family Safety category. In the resulting Parental Controls window (see Figure 14-10), click the user for whom you wish to apply Parental Controls.

2. In the resulting User Controls dialog box (see Figure 14-11), make any of the following settings:

   • Select the On, Enforce Current Settings check box to turn Parental Controls on.

   • Select the On, Collect Information about Computer Usage check box to receive reports about this user's computer activities.

   • Click the Windows Vista Web Filter link to access a form that allows you to specify what type of Web content this user should be allowed to access.

   • Click any of the Settings (Time Limits, Games, Allow and Block Specific Programs, and Activity Reports) to further control how much time can be spent online and what kinds of activities the user can engage in.

3. Click OK and then click the Close button to close the Parental Controls window. The settings take effect the next time the user logs in. If the user is currently logged in, the settings will not take place until he logs off and then logs on again or you restart the computer.

Figure 14-10: The Parental Controls window

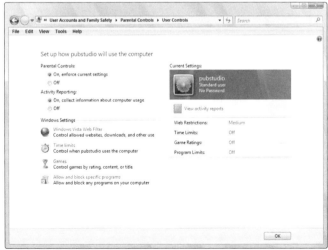

Figure 14-11: The User Controls dialog box

Protecting Windows

*A*fter working with Windows for a while as well as the software that it supports, you build a treasure trove of information and documents. Microsoft provides security features within Windows that help to keep your information private, whether at work or home, and also keep you in safe territory when you're online. You can do the following:

➟ **Set up Internet Explorer zones.** Designate Trusted Web sites (from which you feel perfectly safe downloading files) and Restricted sites (which are likely to contain things that you wouldn't download to your worst enemy's computer).

➟ **Make sure protections are up to date.** By enabling a firewall to keep your computer safe from outsiders and also keeping Windows up to date, you can avoid several kinds of attacks on your data.

➟ **Work with Windows Defender.** New in Windows Vista is *Windows Defender,* which is a built-in solution for protecting you against spyware (typically software downloaded to your computer that causes those nasty pop-ups to appear).

Chapter 15

Get ready to . . .

Set Up Trusted and Restricted Web Sites

1. Double-click the Internet Explorer icon on the Windows desktop or Quick Launch bar to start your browser.

2. Choose Tools⇨Internet Options.

3. In the Internet Options dialog box (see Figure 15-1), click the Security tab.

4. Click the Trusted Sites icon and then click the Sites button.

5. In the resulting Trusted Sites dialog box, enter a URL in the Add This Web Site to the Zone text box for a Web site you want to allow your computer to access.

6. Click Add to add the site to the list of Web sites, as shown in Figure 15-2.

7. Repeat Steps 3–6 to add more sites.

8. When you're done, click Close and then click OK to close the dialog boxes.

9. Repeat Steps 1–8, clicking the Restricted Sites icon rather than Trusted Sites in Step 4 to designate sites that you don't want your computer to access.

 If the Require Server Verification (https:) for All Sites In This Zone check box is selected in the Trusted Sites dialog box, any Trusted site you add must use the `https` prefix, which indicates that the site has a secure connection.

 You can establish a Privacy setting on the Privacy tab of the Internet Options dialog box to control which sites are allowed to download *cookies* to your computer. *Cookies* are tiny files that a site uses to track your online activity and recognize you when you return to the source site. *Trusted sites* are ones that you allow to download cookies to your computer even though the privacy setting you have made might not allow many other sites to do so. *Restricted sites* can never download cookies to your computer, no matter what your privacy setting is.

Figure 15-1: The Internet Options dialog box, Security tab

Figure 15-2: The Trusted Sites dialog box

Enable the Windows Firewall

1. Choose Start➪Control Panel➪Check This Computer's Security Status.

2. In the Windows Security Center window that appears (see Figure 15-3), check that the Windows Firewall is marked as On. If it isn't, click the Windows Firewall link in the left pane of the window and then click the Change Settings link in the resulting dialog box.

3. In the resulting Windows Firewall window (see Figure 15-4), select the On radio button and then click OK.

4. Click the Close button to close Windows Security Center and the Control Panel.

 A *firewall* is a program that protects your computer from the outside world. This is generally a good thing, unless you use a Virtual Private Network (VPN). Using a firewall with a VPN results in you being unable to share files and use some other VPN features.

 Antivirus and security software programs may offer their own firewall protection and may display a message asking if you want to switch. Check their features against Windows and then decide, but usually most firewall features are comparable. The important thing is to have one activated.

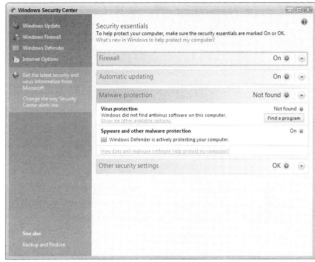

Figure 15-3: The Windows Security Center window

Figure 15-4: The Windows Firewall dialog box

Set Up Windows Defender to Run Automatically

1. Choose Start⇨All Programs⇨Windows Defender.

2. In the resulting Windows Defender window, choose Tools⇨Options. In the Options dialog box that appears (see Figure 15-5), select the Automatically Scan My Computer check box if it's not already selected, and then choose the frequency, time of day, and type of scan from the drop-down lists.

3. To ensure that your scan uses the latest definitions for malware (a kind of spyware with malicious intent), select the Check for Updated Definitions Before Scanning check box.

4. Scroll down to the bottom of the Options dialog box (see Figure 15-6) and make sure that the Use Windows Defender check box is enabled (checked) to activate the program.

5. Click Save to save your settings.

If you want to exclude certain files or locations from the regular scans, you can use the Advanced Options in the Windows Defender dialog box. Click the Add button and browse for the location or file you want to exclude.

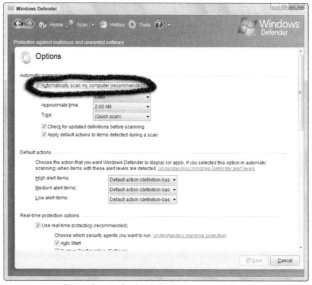

Figure 15-5: The Windows Defender dialog box

Figure 15-6: Turn on Windows Defender in the Administrator Options

Use Windows Defender to Monitor Programs

1. Choose Start⇨All Programs⇨Windows Defender.

2. In the resulting Windows Defender window, choose Tools⇨Software Explorer (see Figure 15-7). In the Software Explorer window that appears, click the Category button and choose a category of software to display.

3. Click any program you'd like to monitor. Detailed information about that program appears (see Figure 15-8).

4. Your options might vary, depending on the category of software you select. For example, for Currently Running Programs, if you want to stop a process in progress, click End Process. If you want to display the Task Manager window to manage specific software tasks, click Task Manager. For Startup Programs, you can use the buttons displayed to remove a program from the startup programs, disable or enable a program, and so on.

5. When you finish working with Software Explorer, click the Close button.

 You can use the information about programs available in Software Explorer to verify program information, such as its publisher, version, when it was installed, and whether it shipped with your operating system. These details might help you verify whether a piece of software on your system is legitimate or one that you'd rather not run.

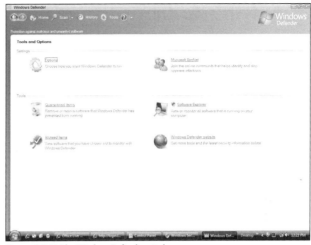

Figure 15-7: The Windows Defender window

Figure 15-8: Software Explorer

Run a Windows Defender Scan

1. Choose Start⇨All Programs⇨Windows Defender.

2. In the resulting Windows Defender window, click the down-arrow on the Scan button (see Figure 15-9). In the resulting menu, choose one of three options:

   - **Quick Scan:** This runs a scan of the likeliest spots on your computer where spyware might lurk. In many cases, this quicker scanning process finds most, if not all, problems and is good choice for a daily automatic scan.

   - **Full Scan:** This scan checks every single file and folder on your computer and gives any currently running programs the once-over. However, be aware that a Full Scan can cause your computer to run a little more slowly while it runs.

   - **Custom Scan:** This scan allows you to customize where to scan. This is helpful if you suspect that a particular drive or folder is harboring a problem.

3. If you choose Quick Scan or Full Scan, the scan begins immediately. If you choose Custom Scan, you can click the Select button in the Select Scan Options dialog box that appears (see Figure 15-10). Then, in the Select Drives and Folders to Scan dialog box, select drives, files, and folders to scan. Click OK. Back in the Select Scan Options dialog box, click Scan Now.

 The History button in Windows Defender gives you a review of the activities and actions taken by Windows Defender. In that window you can also view your settings for Microsoft SpyNet. By default you have joined with a basic membership that reports actions to remove spyware. An advanced membership alerts you when new threats are detected. Allowing reports on spyware activity can help Microsoft prevent or stop such threats, however, if you don't want to report issues with your computer and spyware to Microsoft, you can choose not to join Microsoft SpyNet.

Figure 15-9: The Scan menu in the Windows Defender window

Figure 15-10: The Select Scan Options dialog box

Run Windows Update

1. Choose Start⇨All Programs⇨Windows Update.

2. In the Windows Update window, click Check for Updates. Windows thinks about this for a while, so feel free to page through a magazine for a minute or two.

3. In the resulting window, as shown in Figure 15-11, click the View Available Updates link.

4. In the following window, which shows the available updates (see Figure 15-12), you can click to select updates that you want to install. Then click the Install button.

5. A window appears showing the progress of your installation. When the installation is complete, you might get a message telling you that it's a good idea to restart your computer to complete the installation. Click Restart Now.

 You can set up Windows Update to run at the same time every day. Click the Change Settings link in the Windows Update window and choose the frequency (such as every day) and time of day to check for and install updates.

 Windows Ultimate Extras which is mentioned in the Windows Update window is a program that provides you with programs, services, and content for the Windows Vista Ultimate version of the program. Other versions of Windows Vista cannot sign up for this program.

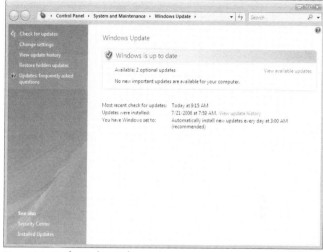

Figure 15-11: The Windows Update window

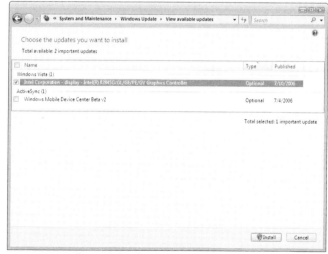

Figure 15-12: Selecting which updates to install

Maintaining Windows

*T*his chapter covers tasks akin to changing the oil in your car: Maintenance might not be a barrel of laughs, but it keeps your car (or in this case, your computer) running, so it has to be done. These are the types of tasks that help you organize, maintain, and protect your computer system.

Windows Vista handles lots and lots of files. To keep your computer and Windows in tip-top shape, you need to organize files in logical ways, perform maintenance activities, prepare for disaster — and know how to recover from it.

The tasks in this chapter fall into three different categories:

➠ **Backing up your files:** Backing up files is a good computing practice, guaranteeing that you have a copy of all your work in case of a crash. You have to use a writable CD or DVD disc to back up files to it.

➠ **Performing basic maintenance:** These tasks are the equivalent of a janitorial service. To keep your system in shape, you can *defragment* your hard drive (take little fragments of files and consolidate them for efficiency) or free up space on the drive. These two tasks troubleshoot files on your hard drive to make sure that you get the best performance from your computer.

➠ **Clearing up clutter:** You can delete cookies and temporary files placed on your computer during online sessions to stop them from cluttering your hard drive. You can also schedule routine maintenance tasks to happen automatically so you don't take a chance that you forget to perform them.

Chapter 16

Get ready to . . .

Back Up Files to a Writable CD or DVD

1. Place a blank writable CD R/RW (read/writable) or DVD R/RW in your CD-ROM or DVD-ROM drive and then choose Start⇨Documents.

2. In the resulting Documents window (see Figure 16-1), select all the files that you want to copy to disc.

3. Right-click the files that you want and then choose Send To⇨*Name of your writable CD-R/RW-ROM or DVD-ROM drive.*

4. In the Burn a Disc dialog box that appears, enter a disc title and choose whether you wish to change the file format selection. Click Next.

5. In the window that appears (see Figure 16-2), click Burn to Disc. When the files have been copied, click the Close button to close the CD-R/RW-ROM or DVD-ROM window.

 If you want to back up the entire contents of a folder, such as the Document folder, you can just click the Documents folder itself in Step 2.

 You can also back up to a network or another drive by using the Back Up Your Computer link in the Control Panel. Using Windows Backup, you can make settings to regularly back up to a local disk or CD R/RW/DVD drive, or to a network. Backing up to a CD/DVD is a little different from burning a disc in that after you back up your files, only changes are saved each subsequent time a backup is run.

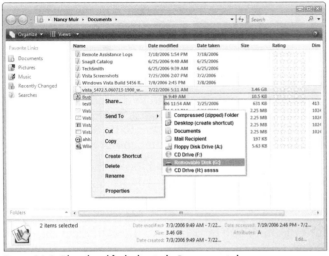

Figure 16-1: Files selected for backup in the Documents window

Figure 16-2: Files waiting to be copied to a writable CD

Defragment a Hard Drive

1. Choose Start⇨Control Panel⇨System and Maintenance and then click Defragment Your Hard Drive in the Administrative Tools.

2. In the resulting Disk Defragmenter window (see Figure 16-3), to the left of the Defragment Now button is a note about whether your system requires defragmenting. If it does, click Defragment Now. A message appears (see Figure 16-4) that Windows is defragmenting your drive and that it may take up to a few hours to complete.

3. When the defragmenting process is complete, the Disk Defragmenter window shows that your drive no longer requires defragmenting. Click Close to close the window.

 Warning: Disk defragmenting could take a while. If you have energy-saving features active (such as a screen saver), they could cause the defragmenter to stop and start all over again. Try running your defrag overnight while you're happily dreaming of much more interesting things. You can also set up the procedure to run automatically at a preset period of time, such as once every two weeks by using the Run Automatically setting in the Disk Defragmenter window.

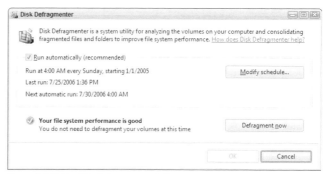

Figure 16-3: The Disk Defragmenter window

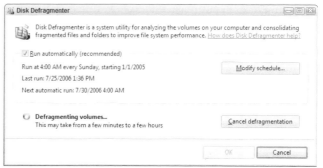

Figure 16-4: The Disk Defragmenter in action

Free Disk Space

1. Choose Start⇨Control Panel⇨System and Maintenance and then click Free Up Disk Space in the Administrative Tools.

2. In the dialog box that appears (see Figure 16-5), click the icon next to the kind of files you want to clean up. If you choose All Files on This Computer, go to Step 3. If you choose My Files Only, choose the drives you want to scan from the Disk Cleanup: Drive Selection dialog box that appears.

3. The resulting dialog box shown in Figure 16-6 tells you that Disk Cleanup calculated how much space can be cleared on your hard drive and displays the suggested files to delete in a list (those to be deleted have a check mark). If you want to select additional files in the list to delete, click to place a check mark next to them.

4. After you select all the files to delete, click OK. The selected files are deleted.

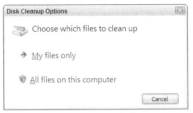

Figure 16-5: Choose your Disk Cleanup option

Figure 16-6: The Disk Cleanup dialog box

 Click the View Files button in the Disk Cleanup dialog box to see more details about the files that Windows proposes to delete, including the size of the files and when they were created or last accessed.

 If you can't free up enough disk space for your needs you might consider running Error Checking to locate bad sectors on your hard drive, covered in Chapter 17 or even replacing your hard drive with one that has more capacity.

Delete Temporary Internet Files by Using Internet Explorer

1. Open Internet Explorer.

2. Choose Tools⇨Internet Options.

3. On the General tab of the resulting Internet Options dialog box (see Figure 16-7), click the Delete button in the Browsing History section.

4. In the resulting Delete Browsing History dialog box, as shown in Figure 16-8, click the Delete Files button in the Temporary Internet Files section.

5. A confirmation message asks whether you want to delete the files. Click Yes. Click Close and then click OK to close the open dialog boxes.

Temporary Internet files can be deleted when you run Disk Cleanup (see that task earlier in this chapter), but the process that I describe here allows you to delete them without having to make choices about deleting other files on your system.

Windows Vista offers a new feature for rating and improving your computer's performance. From the System and Maintenance category in the Control Panel, click the Check Your Computer's Windows Experience Index Base Score. In the resulting dialog box click the Refresh Now button to get a rating of your processor speed, memory operations, and more.

Figure 16-7: The Internet Options dialog box

Figure 16-8: The Delete Browsing History dialog box

Delete Cookies by Using Internet Explorer

1. Open Internet Explorer.

2. Choose Tools➪Internet Options.

3. On the General tab of the resulting Internet Options dialog box (see Figure 16-9), click the Delete button in the Browsing History section.

4. In the resulting dialog box, as shown in Figure 16-10, click the Delete Cookies button in the Cookies section.

5. A confirmation message asks whether you want to delete the files. Click Yes. Click Close and then click OK to close the open dialog boxes.

 There are pros and cons to allowing cookies to be saved on your computer. Cookies embed information about you and your Internet browsing habits on your computer which Web sites can use to predict your buying interests. That information can be used to push annoying pop-up windows at you, or simply suggest products you might be interested in buying when you revisit a favorite online store. If you don't want to have cookies saved to your computer change privacy a higher setting (see Chapter 7 for more about this).

Figure 16-9: The Internet Options dialog box

Figure 16-10: The Delete Browsing History dialog box

Schedule Maintenance Tasks

1. Choose Start⇨Control Panel⇨System and Maintenance and then click Schedule Tasks in the Administrative Tools.

2. In the resulting Task Scheduler dialog box, as shown in Figure 16-11, choose Action⇨Create Task.

3. In the resulting Create Task dialog box, enter a task name and description. Choose when to run the task (only when you are logged on, or whether you're logged in or not).

4. Click the Triggers tab and then click New. In the New Trigger dialog box, choose a criteria in the Begin the Task drop-down list and use the Settings to specify how often to perform the task as well as when and at what time of day to begin. Click OK.

5. Click the Actions tab and then click New. In the New Action dialog box, choose the action that will occur from the Action drop-down list. These include starting a program, sending an e-mail, or displaying a message. Depending on what you choose here, different action dialog boxes appear. For example, if you want to send an e-mail, you get an e-mail form to fill in.

6. If you want to set conditions in addition to those that trigger the action that control whether it should occur, click the Conditions tab and enter them.

7. In the resulting dialog box, select a start time and start date by clicking the arrows in each field. Then click Next.

8. Click the Settings tab and make settings that control how the task runs.

9. After you complete all settings, click OK to save the task.

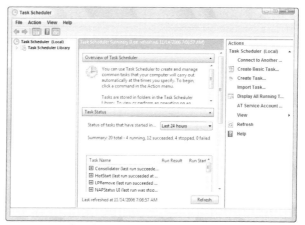

Figure 16-11: The Task Scheduler dialog box

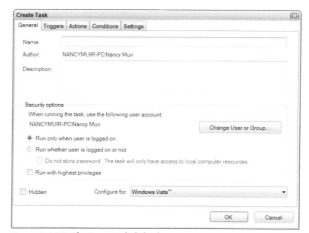

Figure 16-12: The Create Task dialog box

 If you like a more wizard-like interface for building a new task, you can choose the Create Basic Task item from the Action menu. This walks you through the most basic and minimal settings you can make to create a new task.

Part VI
Fixing Common Problems

The 5th Wave   By Rich Tennant

"How's the defragmentation coming?"

Troubleshooting Hardware Problems

C omputer hardware, like your CPU and printer, is cool. *Hardware* is the gadgetry that hums and beeps and looks neat on your desktop. But when hardware goes wrong, you might be tempted to throw it out the window. Don't do that — think of all the money you spent on it. Instead, use Windows to isolate and troubleshoot the problem.

Windows Vista has several features that help you diagnose and treat the sickest hardware, including

➡ A method of checking whether your printer model is compatible with Windows Vista.

➡ A Disk Cleanup feature that checks your hard drive for problems that could be causing poor performance, such as bad sectors on the drive or bits of stray data that could simply be thrown away — and then freeing space and helping your system to perform better.

➡ Modem diagnostics that query your modem to be sure that it's connected, configured, and performing properly.

➡ A Hardware Troubleshooter feature in the Windows Help and Support Center that offers advice to help you fix a variety of hardware problems.

➡ The ability to quickly and easily update hardware drivers that might help your hardware perform optimally or revert to a previous driver if a newer version is causing problems.

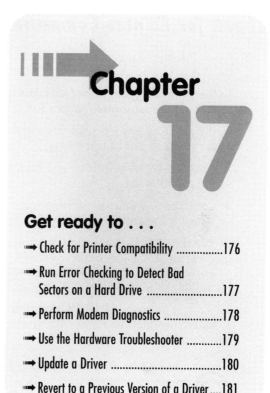

Chapter 17

Get ready to . . .

Check for Printer Compatibility

1. Open Internet Explorer and go to `http://testedproducts.windowsmarketplace.com`.

2. In the window that appears (see Figure 17-1), click Printers in the hardware category list.

3. In the resulting Printers page (see Figure 17-2), locate your printer in one of three ways:

   - Click a category of printer and find your printer in the resulting list.

   - Click the manufacturer company for your printer and locate your printer in the resulting list.

   - Use the alphabetical listing of printers. (Note that there are 436 pages of these listings, so click the Sort By field and page links at the top to get to your model name.)

4. When you locate your model of printer, click it to see detailed information about what versions of Windows it is compatible with.

 Beyond being compatible with Windows Vista, here are some sneaky printer problems to look for: The printer isn't connected to the computer; the printer isn't plugged in; the printer driver is out of date; the printer doesn't have an ink cartridge in it; the printer isn't set up as the current printer (so you're printing to some other printer or trying to print to a printer that's no longer connected to your computer); or the printer lid is open.

 You can also find a link to the Windows Tested Products List Web site through the Troubleshooting section of Help and Support, in the Hardware and Drivers section.

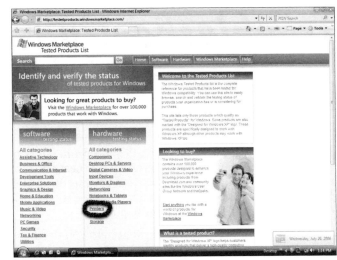

Figure 17-1: The Windows Tested Products page

Figure 17-2: The Printers page

Run Error Checking to Detect Bad Sectors on a Hard Drive

1. Choose Start⇨Computer.

2. Right-click the drive you want to repair and then choose Properties.

3. In the resulting Properties dialog box, click the Tools tab to display it (see Figure 17-3). Then click the Check Now button.

4. In the resulting Check Disk dialog box (see Figure 17-4), choose the option you want to use:

   - **Automatically Fix File System Errors:** You have to close all files in order to run this option.

   - **Scan For and Attempt Recovery of Bad Sectors:** If you select this option, it also automatically fixes any errors found, so you don't need to select the first option as well.

5. Click Start.

 If there are unrecoverable sectors that can't be fixed by using this utility, they will be flagged so that Windows doesn't attempt to access them anymore.

Figure 17-3: The Properties dialog box, Tools tab

Figure 17-4: The Check Disk dialog box

Perform Modem Diagnostics

1. Choose Start➪Control Panel➪Hardware and Sound and then click Device Manager.

2. In the resulting window, click the plus sign next to Modems to display installed modems. Right-click a modem and choose Properties from the shortcut menu.

3. On the Diagnostics tab of the resulting Modem Properties dialog box (see Figure 17-5), click Query Modem.

4. What appears at this point differs depending on whether the modem is experiencing a problem. If the modem is working properly, the response reads Success (see Figure 17-6 for an example). You can select the Append to Log check box to add this information to your log, and then share the log with a technical support person to get help with your modem problem.

5. Click OK and then click the Close button on the Device Manager window.

6. Find the problem and click the Close button in the upper-right corner of the Troubleshooter to close it.

 You should also check the Resource tab of the Modem Properties dialog box, which lists any other devices on your system that might be in conflict with your modem and therefore cause problems. Disable those devices and try your modem again.

 If the modem isn't working properly, try the troubleshooting feature of the Help and Support window to try to pinpoint the problem.

Figure 17-5: The Modem Properties dialog box, Diagnostics tab

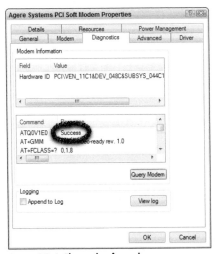

Figure 17-6: The results of a modem query

Use the Hardware Troubleshooter

1. Choose Start⇨Help and Support⇨Troubleshooting.

2. In the resulting Troubleshooting in Windows window, scroll down the Hardware and Drivers section, and click the Troubleshoot Driver Problems link (see Figure 17-7).

3. Follow the instructions that relate to your problem. (Figure 17-8 shows things to try if your device used to work but now doesn't, as an example.)

4. After you solve the problem, click the Close button to close the Troubleshooting window. If you don't find a solution, consider using the Remote Assistance feature to get one-on-one help (see Chapter 19 for more about this feature).

 You might also find help with hardware drivers by going to the Device Manager (Start⇨Control Panel⇨Hardware and Sound⇨Device Manager) and right-clicking a device. Choose Properties and then display the Driver tab to update or test a driver.

 The In This Article listing of links helps you pinpoint the information you want to find in the Troubleshooter feature. The Get Help from Other People link may also lead you to resources who can help with your troubleshooting tasks.

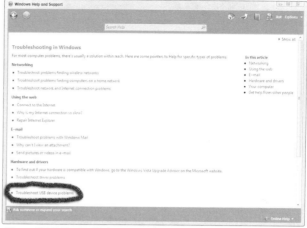

Figure 17-7: The Troubleshooting window

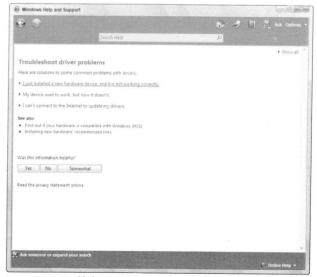

Figure 17-8: Troubleshooting advice

Update a Driver

1. Choose Start⇨Help and Support.

2. In the resulting Help and Support window click Table of Contents, then click Hardware, Devices, and Drivers, and finally click Driver Software. In the Driver Software window, click Repair or Update a Driver.

3. In the resulting Repair or Update a Driver window (see Figure 17-9), click the To Update Driver Software Using Windows Update link, click the Click to Open Windows Update link, and follow the instructions (see Figure 17-10).

4. When you finish updating the driver, click the Close button to close the Windows Help and Support window.

 In some cases, you have to reboot your computer to give Windows a chance to load the new driver. Choose Start⇨Turn Off Computer. In the resulting Turn Off Computer dialog box, click the Restart button to reboot your system. The driver should now, by the magic of the Windows Plug and Play feature that automatically detects new hardware, be working.

 If you don't find the updated driver using the Windows Vista procedure outlined above, consider going directly to the hardware manufacturer's Web site and downloading the latest driver.

Figure 17-9: The Repair or Update a Driver window

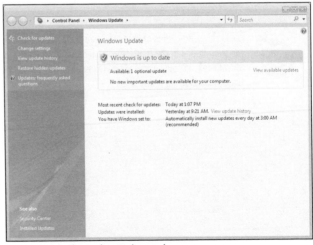

Figure 17-10: The Windows Update window

Revert to a Previous Version of a Driver

1. Disconnect the device that's associated with the driver that's causing trouble.

2. Turn off the device.

3. Choose Start➪Control Panel➪Hardware and Sound and click the Update Device Drivers link in the Device Manager category.

4. In the resulting Device Manager window, click the arrow to the left of a category of device to display the devices, and then right-click on the device you want to rollback and choose Properties.

5. In the resulting Properties window (see Figure 17-11), click the Driver tab and then click the Roll Back Driver button.

> There's another option for updating a driver. On the Driver tab of the device Properties dialog box, click the Uninstall button to remove the driver. You can then install a new one from a disc or by downloading it over the Internet.

Figure 17-11: The Properties window for a device

Troubleshooting Software Problems

All the wonderful hardware that you've spent your hard-earned money on doesn't mean a thing if the software driving it goes flooey. If any programs cause your system to *crash* (meaning it freezes up so there's less action on your screen than on a loser's prom night), you can try a variety of tasks to fix it. In this chapter, you find out how to recover when the following problems occur:

➠ When a program crashes, you can simply shut down that program by using the Windows Task Manager. This utility keeps track of all the programs and processes that are running on your computer.

➠ If you've got problems and Windows isn't responding, sometimes it helps to restart in Safe Mode, which requires only basic files and drivers. Restarting in Safe Mode often allows you to troubleshoot what's going on, and you can restart Windows in its regular mode after the problem is solved.

➠ Use the System Restore feature to first create a *system restore point* (a point in time when your settings and programs all seem to be humming along just fine) and then restore Windows to that point when trouble hits.

➠ If all else fails, you might have to reformat an entire drive. This wipes all information from the drive. If it's the hard drive that you reformat, you have to start again by reloading the operating system and all your software.

➠ Sometimes you just have to run older programs on Windows Vista. To avoid compatibility issues that could crash your system, try running the Program Compatibility Wizard to test your program first.

Chapter 18

Get ready to . . .

Shut Down a Nonresponsive Application

1. Press Ctrl+Alt+Del.

2. In the Windows screen that appears, click Start Task Manager.

3. In the resulting Windows Task Manager dialog box (see Figure 18-1), select the application that you were in when your system stopped responding.

4. Click the End Task button.

5. In the resulting dialog box, the Windows Task Manager tells you that the application isn't responding and asks whether you want to shut it down now. Click Yes.

Figure 18-1: The Windows Task Manager

 If pressing Ctrl+Alt+Del doesn't bring up the Task Manager, you're in bigger trouble than you thought. You might need to press and hold your computer power button to shut down. Note that some applications use an AutoSave feature that keeps an interim version of the document that you were working in — you might be able to save some of your work by opening that last-saved version. Other programs don't have such a safety net, and you simply lose whatever changes you made to your document since the last time you saved it. The moral? Save, and save often.

 You may see a dialog box appear when an application shuts down that asks if you want to report the problem to Microsoft. In the past if you said yes, information went to Microsoft and that's the last you heard of it. In Windows Vista you actually get a message back with suggestions on how to solve the problem. This message appears in a little window on your screen.

Start Windows in Safe Mode

1. Remove any CDs or DVDs from your computer.

2. Choose Start, click the arrow on the right of the Lock button, and then choose Restart to reboot your system (see Figure 18-2).

3. When the computer starts to reboot (the screen goes black), begin pressing F8.

4. If you have more than one operating system, you might see the Windows Advanced Options menu. Use the up- and down-arrow keys to select the Windows Vista operating system. Or, type the number of that choice, press Enter, and then continue to press F8.

5. In the resulting plain-vanilla text-based screen, press the up- or down-arrow key to select the Safe Mode option from the list and then press Enter.

6. Log in to your computer with administrator privileges; a Safe Mode screen appears (see Figure 18-3). Use the tools in the Control Panel and the Help and Support system to figure out your problem, make changes, and then restart. When you restart again (repeat Step 2), let your computer start in the standard Windows Vista mode.

 When you reboot and press F8 as in Step 2, you're in the old text-based world that users of the DOS operating system will remember. It's scary out there! Your mouse doesn't work a lick, and no fun sounds or cool graphics exist to sooth you. In fact, DOS is the reason the whole *For Dummies* series started because *everybody* felt like a dummy using it, me included. Just use your arrow keys to get around and press Enter to make selections. You're back in Windows-land soon . . .

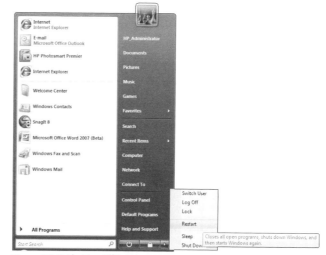

Figure 18-2: The Turn Off Computer menu

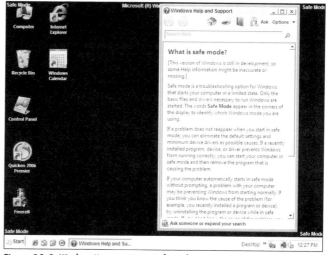

Figure 18-3: Windows Vista running in Safe Mode

Create a System Restore Point

1. Choose Start⇨Control Panel⇨Backup Your Computer (under System and Maintenance).

2. In the Backup and Restore Center window, click Create a Restore Point or Change Settings under Tasks. The User Account Control might display a dialog box asking for your permission to continue; if so, click Continue.

3. On the System Protection tab of the System Properties dialog box that appears (see Figure 18-4), click Create.

4. In the resulting Create a Restore Point dialog box (see Figure 18-5), enter a description; this description is helpful if you create multiple restore points and want to identify the correct one. The current date is usually your best bet.

5. Click the Create button, and the system restore point is created and is available to you when you run a System Restore. (See the following task for more about this.)

6. In the dialog box that appears telling you the restore point was created successfully, click OK and then click OK again to close the Control Panel.

 Every once in a while, when you install some software, make some new settings in Windows, and things seem to be running just fine, create a system restore point. It's good computer practice, just like backing up your files, only you're backing up your settings. Once a month or once every couple months works for most people, but if you frequently make changes, create a system restore point more often.

 A more drastic option to System Restore is to run the system recovery disc that probably came with your computer or that you created using discs you provided. However, system recovery essentially puts your computer right back to the configuration it had when it was carried out of the factory. That means you lose any software you've installed and documents you've created since you began to use it. A good argument for creating system restore points on a regular basis, don't you think?

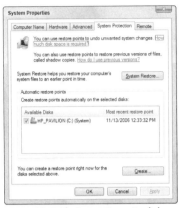

Figure 18-4: The System Properties dialog box, System Protection tab

Figure 18-5: The Create a Restore Point dialog box

Restore the Windows System

1. Choose Start⇨Control Panel⇨Back Up Your Computer (under System and Maintenance).

2. In the Backup and Restore Center window, click Repair Windows Using System Restore in the Tasks list.

3. In the resulting System Restore dialog box (see Figure 18-6), click Next. In the next window that appears, as shown in Figure 18-7, click Finish to confirm the system restore point.

4. A dialog box confirms that you want to run System Restore. Click Yes.

5. The system goes through a shutdown and restart sequence, and then displays a dialog box that informs you that the System Restore has occurred.

6. Click OK to close it.

 System Restore doesn't get rid of files that you've saved, so you don't lose your Ph.D. dissertation. System Restore simply reverts to Windows settings as of the restore point. This can help if you or some piece of installed software made a setting that is causing some conflict in your system that makes your computer sluggish or prone to crashes.

 System Restore doesn't always solve the problem. You very best bet is to be sure you create a set of backup discs for your computer when you buy it. If you didn't do that, and you can't get things running right again, contact your computer manufacturer. They may be able to send you a set of recovery discs, though they may charge a small fee. These discs restore your computer to its state when it left the factory, and in this case you lose applications you installed and documents you created, but you get your computer running again.

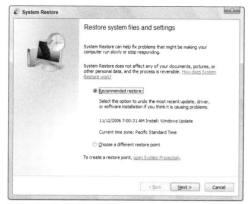

Figure 18-6: The System Restore dialog box

Figure 18-7: Confirming the restore point to use

Reformat a Drive

1. Assuming your system is still functional enough to let you do so, back up everything you can find (documents, photos, graphics, saved e-mails, updates, drivers, and so on; don't worry about software programs because you'll have to reinstall those, anyway) and close all applications.

2. Choose Start⇨Control Panel⇨System and Maintenance⇨Administrative Tools.

3. In the Administrative Tools window (see Figure 18-8), double-click the Computer Management link.

4. In the resulting Computer Management window, click the Disk Management link on the left. In the resulting window (see Figure 18-9), right-click the drive or partition that you want to reformat, and then choose Format from the shortcut menu that appears.

5. In the resulting dialog box, select the options you want (file system and size) and then click OK.

The two file systems types that you can choose from are NTFS and FAT32. NTFS, which stands for NT File System, is the default. This format supports long filenames, and various storage, security, and recovery features of Windows NT. FAT32 is an older system used by the now antiquated MS-DOS to organize files. You are probably better off leaving NTFS as your file system choice.

Note that you have to be logged on as the head honcho — the system administrator — to perform these steps. And it's worth repeating: Reformatting a drive wipes *everything* off it, so be sure that's what you want to do before you do it.

I can't stress this strongly enough: Before you reformat a drive, you should back up everything you can, including drivers or updates to software that you've sat through tedious minutes (or hours) to download from the Web. You don't want to have to spend all that download time all over again to get yourself up to speed.

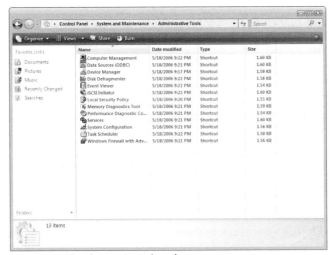

Figure 18-8: The Administrative Tools window

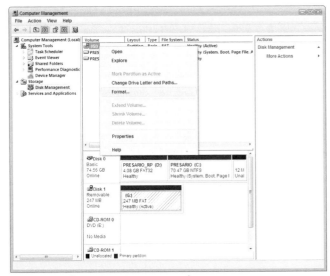

Figure 18-9: The Computer Management window

Getting Help

*W*ith so many Windows Vista features, you're bound to run into something that doesn't work right or isn't easy to figure out (or that this book doesn't cover). That's when you need to call on the resources that Microsoft provides to help you out.

Through the Help and Support Center, you can get help in various ways, including the following:

➡ **Access information that's stored in the Help system database.** Drill down from one topic to another or by using a powerful search mechanism. There's even a troubleshooting feature that helps you pin down your problem.

➡ **Get help from your fellow Windows users.** Tap into information exchanged by users in Windows Communities or by using a little feature called *Remote Assistance*, which allows you to let another user take over your computer from a distance (via the Internet) and figure out your problem for you.

➡ **Bite the bullet and pay for it.** Microsoft offers some help for free (for example, help for installing its software that you paid good money for), but some help comes for a price. When you can't find help anywhere else, you might want to consider forking over a few hard-earned bucks for this option.

|||➡ **Chapter**

19

Get ready to . . .

Explore the Help Table of Contents

1. Choose Start➪Help and Support to open Windows Help and Support, as shown in Figure 19-1. *Note:* If your copy of Windows came built into your computer, some computer manufacturers (such as Hewlett-Packard), customize this center to add information that's specific to your computer system.

2. Click the Table of Contents link to display a list of topics. Click any of the topics to see a list of subtopics. Eventually, you get down to the deepest level of detailed subtopics that have question mark icons next to them, as shown in Figure 19-2.

3. Click a subtopic to read its contents. Some subtopics contain blue links that lead to related topics. Links with a green arrow next to them perform an action when clicked, such as opening a dialog box so you can complete a task.

4. Click any words in green to view a definition of those terms. When you finish reading a help topic, click the Close button to close the Help and Support window.

You can click the Print icon in the set of tools at the top right of the Help and Support window to print any displayed topic. You can also click the Restore Down button in the title bar to minimize the window and keep it available while you work in your computer.

It helps you to get the most up-to-date help information if you are connected to the Internet when you open Help and Support. If you are not connected you can still browse the database of help information installed with Windows Vista, but you will see a message in the help window telling you you are not connected.

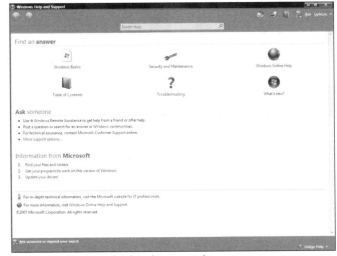

Figure 19-1: The Microsoft Help and Support window

Figure 19-2: Detailed level help subtopics

Search for Help

1. Open the Help and Support Window.

2. Enter a search term in the Search box and then click the Search Help button. Search results, such as those shown in Figure 19-3, appear.

3. Explore the results by clicking various links in the Search Results. These links offer a few different types of results:

   - Clicking a link with a right-pointing triangle displays steps or additional information.

   - Clicking a link with a green arrow next to it performs an action, such as opening a dialog box.

   - Clicking a See Also link at the bottom of the search results takes you to a help topic.

   - In some search results, an article is displayed with an index of topics titled In This Article (see Figure 19-4).

4. If you have no luck, enter a different search term in the Search text box and start again.

 If you don't find what you need with Search, consider clicking the Browse Help button in the top right of the Help and Support window (it sports a little blue icon in the shape of a book) to display a list of major topics. Those topics may also give you some ideas for good search terms to continue your search.

Figure 19-3: The result of a search for the keyword *joystick*

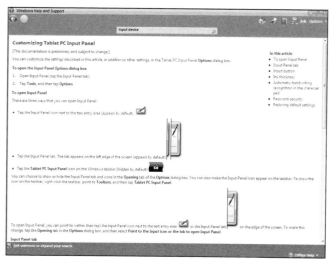

Figure 19-4: An article displayed from a search

Post a Question in Windows Communities

1. Open the Help and Support Center. Then, in the Ask Someone section of the main help page, click the Windows Communities link.

2. In the Microsoft Windows Vista Newsgroups page that opens in your browser (see Figure 19-5), enter a keyword in the Search For field. Then, from the In drop-down list, choose which newsgroup to search in.

3. In the resulting Search Results page, click to display a list of all replies under it. Click an item to display it in the lower pane (see Figure 19-6).

4. Perform any of the following actions to participate in the newsgroup. (*Note:* You have to click Sign In and enter your Microsoft Passport information to participate in the discussion.)

   - **Update your profile.** Click the Edit My Profile button to enter your display name and any other information you want to appear about you when you post a message.

   - **Post a new message.** Choose New⇨Question, select the discussion group to participate in, and then enter the Subject and Message in their respective text boxes. Click to accept the terms of use, and then click Post to post your question.

   - **Reply to a message in a discussion.** With the list of postings and replies displayed, click the Reply button, fill in the message, and then click Post.

 You can also use the Search feature to search for keywords or phrases in discussions. Enter a word or phrase in the Search text box, select a discussion to search in the In drop-down list, and then click Go. Relevant messages are displayed; click one to read it.

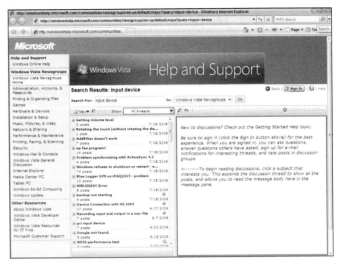

Figure 19-5: The Windows Vista Newsgroup page

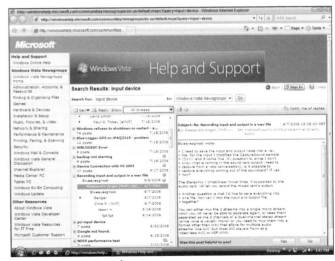

Figure 19-6: A newsgroup discussion page

Access Windows Online Help

1. Open the Help and Support Center and then click the Windows Online Help icon.

2. In the window that appears (see Figure 19-7), you can use links and icons to access the following features:

    *   Click a **Find Answers** icon to find support in categories such as Hardware and Drivers, Printing, and Networking (see Figure 19-8).

    *   Use the links in the **Expert Advice** section to read articles and frequently asked questions about common help topics.

    *   Click the **Get Answers from Other Windows** users link to access Windows Vista Newsgroups. (See the preceding task for information about posting messages in these online communities.)

3. Click the Close button to close the online help window in your browser, and then click the Close button to close Windows Help and Support.

 To set up Help and Support to always Get Online Help, click the arrow on the Online Help button in the bottom-right corner of the Help and Support window, choose Settings, and be sure the check box labelled Include Windows Online Help and Support When You Search for Help is selected.

 The tools on this site change frequently, so these steps might not be totally accurate.

Figure 19-7: The Windows Vista Online Help page

Figure 19-8: The Printing category of online help topics

Connect to Remote Assistance

1. First enable Remote Assistance by choosing Start↪ Control Panel↪System and Maintenance↪System↪ Remote Settings. On the Remote tab, select the Allow Remote Assistance Connections to this Computer check box, and then click OK.

2. Open the Help and Support Center. Click the Windows Remote Assistance link in the Ask Someone area of the Help and Support Center.

3. On the Windows Remote Assistance page, as shown in Figure 19-9, click the Invite Someone You Trust to Help You link. On the page that appears, you can notify somebody that you want help.

4. You can use Windows Messenger or e-mail to invite somebody to help you. For these steps, click Use E-mail to Send an Invitation.

5. Enter and retype a password and click Next. Your default e-mail program opens with an invitation message prepared. Fill in an e-mail address and, if you like, a personal message at the end of the automatically generated invitation. (For example, you might want to provide the password you assigned here.) Click Send.

6. In the resulting Windows Remote Assistance window, as shown in Figure 19-10, when an incoming connection is made, use the tools here to adjust settings, chat, send a file, or pause, cancel, or stop sharing.

7. When you're finished, click the Close button to close the Windows Remote Assistance window.

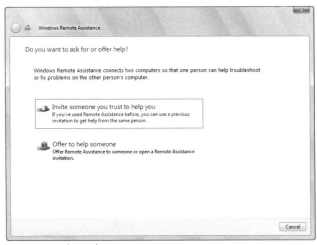

Figure 19-9: The Windows Remote Assistance page

Figure 19-10: Tools to control a Remote Assistance session

 Setting a time limit to not more than a few hours is a good idea. After all, you don't want somebody trying to log on to your computer unexpectedly two weeks from now when you've already solved the problem some other way.

 Remember that it's up to you to let the recipient know the password — it isn't included in your e-mail unless you add it. Although using a password used to be optional in Windows XP, it's mandatory in Windows Vista, and the password you use must be at least six characters long.

Change Help and Support Center Display Options

1. Open the Help and Support Center.

2. Choose Options⇨Text Size and then choose one of the text size options: Largest, Larger, Medium (the default), Smaller, or Smallest (see Figure 19-11).

3. Your new settings take effect immediately; click the Close button or navigate to another area of the Help and Support Center.

 If you don't like the colors in your Help and Support screen you can change them by choosing a different color scheme in the Control Panel, Appearance and Personalization settings.

 Don't forget that you can reduce the size of the display by clicking the Restore Down button in the upper-right corner of the window. This is especially useful with the Help window so you can display it side by side with an application or Control Panel window where you're trying to troubleshoot the described help topic.

Figure 19-11: The Help and Support Center Options menu

Contact Microsoft Customer Support

1. Go to the Help and Support window and click the Ask button in the upper-right corner. On the page that appears, as shown in Figure 19-12, click Windows Communities to post a question online.

2. Click the Microsoft Customer Support link for help with so-called "non-technical" issues, such as subscriptions, events, or training. The Contact Us Web page shown in Figure 19-13 appears.

 Typically, you can call support for two free help sessions or unlimited installation support by submitting a request via e-mail support or calling 866-234-6020. You can get paid phone support for $35 per request by calling 800-936-5700, or advanced support for $245 by calling 800-936-4900. Advanced support is for what Microsoft refers to as *mission critical* issues, dealing with software deployment across an enterprise or larger network issues.

 There is also a live chat support feature through customer support. This is sometimes the quickest way to get somebody's attention, and you get the same two free support calls and unlimited installation support. If your product wasn't purchased as a separate package but through a licensing sale or bundled on a new computer, you have to follow specific instructions on the Customer Support Web page to get product support.

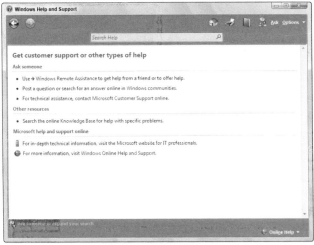

Figure 19-12: The Microsoft Customer Support link

Figure 19-13: A variety of customer support options on the Contact Us Web page

Part VII
Fun and Games

The 5th Wave   By Rich Tennant

"Ms. Gretsky, tell the employees they can have internet games on their computers again."

Playing Games in Windows Vista

All work and no play is just wrong no matter how you look at it. So, Microsoft has built plenty of games into Windows Vista to keep you amused.

Many computer games are essentially virtual versions of games that you already know, such as Solitaire and Chess. But Windows Vista has added some interesting treats to the mix — several that depend to a great extent on some neat onscreen animation.

Altogether, you can access nine games through Windows, and this chapter gives you a sampling of the best of them. Here's what you can expect:

➡ Traditional card games, such as Solitaire and Hearts.

➡ Games of dexterity, such as Minesweeper, where the goal is to be the fastest, smartest clicker in the West.

➡ A game that's great for small children — Purble Place — where the object is to place features on a cartoon character's face that match up.

This chapter also covers setting up a gaming joystick as well as selecting a game rating system that allows you to pick and choose the games you want your family to play.

Chapter 20

Get ready to . . .

Play Solitaire

1. Choose Start➪Games. In the resulting Games window, (see Figure 20-1), double-click Solitaire.

2. In the resulting Solitaire window, click a card (see Figure 20-2) and then click a card in another deck that you want to move it on top of. The first card you click moves.

3. When playing the game, you have the following options:

    *   If no moves are available, click the stack of cards in the upper-left corner to deal another round of cards.

    *   If you move the last card from one of the six laid-out stacks, leaving only face-down cards, click the face-down cards to flip one up. You can also move a King onto any empty stack.

    *   When you reach the end of the stack of cards in the upper-left corner, click them again to redeal the cards that you didn't use the first time.

    *   You can play a card in one of two places: either building a stack from King to Ace on the bottom row, alternating suits; or starting from Ace in any of the top four slots, placing cards from Ace to King in a single suit.

    *   When you complete a set of cards (Ace to King), click the top card and then click one of the four blank deck spots at the top-right of the window. If you complete all four sets, you win.

4. To deal a new game, choose Game➪New Game. Unlike life, it's easy to start over with Solitaire!

5. To close Solitaire, click the Close button.

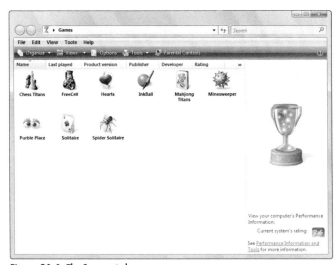

Figure 20-1: The Games window

Figure 20-2: The Solitaire game window

Play FreeCell

1. Choose Start➪Games; in the Games window, double-click FreeCell.

2. In the resulting FreeCell window, as shown in Figure 20-3, a game is ready to play. If you want a fresh game, you can always choose Game➪New Game; a new game is dealt and ready to play.

     The goal is to move all the cards, grouped by the four suits, to the home cells (the four cells in the upper-right corner) stacked in order from Ace at the bottom to King at the top. The trick here is that you get four free cells (the four cells in the upper-left corner) where you can manually move a card out of the way to free up a move. You can also use those four slots to allow you to move up to four cards in a stack at once. (For example, if you want to move a Jack, 10, 9, and 8 all together onto a Queen.) You can move only as many cards as there are free cells available plus one. Free spaces in the rows of card stacks also act as free cells. You win when you have four stacks of cards for each of the four suits placed on the home cells.

3. Click a card; to move it, click a free cell or another card at the bottom of a column. Figure 20-4 shows a game where two free cells are already occupied.

     If you move a card to a free cell, you can move it back to the bottom of a column, but only on a card one higher in an alternate color. You could move a 3 of hearts to a 4 of spades, for example. You stack the cards in the columns in alternating colors, but the cards in the home cells end up in order and all in one suit.

     If you get hooked on this game, try going to www. freecell.com, a Web site devoted to FreeCell. Here you can engage in live games with other players, read more about the rules and strategies, and even buy FreeCell merchandise. Don't say I didn't warn you about the possibility of addiction.

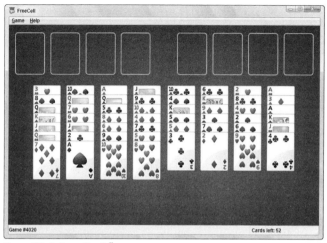

Figure 20-3: A new FreeCell game

Figure 20-4: Occupied cells

Play Spider Solitaire

1. Choose Start⇨Games; in the Games window, double-click Spider Solitaire. A window appears where you can click the level of difficulty you prefer.

2. In the resulting window, click a card and click another card or drag it to the bottom of another stack or to an empty stack so that you match the same suit in each stack, moving in descending order from King to Ace (see Figure 20-5).

3. Move a card to automatically turn over a new card in the stack.

4. After you complete a set of cards in a suit, those cards are moved off the game area. The goal is to remove all the cards in the fewest moves. You can

   - **Deal a new set of cards.** Choose Game⇨New Game or click the stack of cards in the bottom-right corner to deal a new set of cards. (*Note:* You have to have a card on each of the ten stacks before you can deal new ones.)

   - **Save your game.** Choose Game⇨Exit and then click Save in the Exit Game dialog box to save your game.

   - **Change the options.** Choose Game⇨Options (see Figure 20-6) and select a new difficulty level. Other options mainly affect how or whether you save games and open them to continue, and whether the variously annoying or angelic sounds play when you click a card, deal a card, or fold a stack (assuming your computer system is set up with a sound card and speakers).

5. When you finish playing, click the Close button and either click Save or Don't Save in the Exit Game dialog box.

Figure 20-5: The Spider Solitaire game window

Figure 20-6: The Spider Options dialog box

 Stuck for a move? Try choosing Game⇨Hint. Various combinations of cards are highlighted in sequence to suggest a likely next step in the game. If you're not stuck but just bored with the appearance of the game, choose Game⇨Change Appearance and select another desktop and background style.

Play Minesweeper

1. Choose Start⇨Games; in the Games window, double-click Minesweeper. A window appears where you can click the level of difficulty you prefer.

2. The Minesweeper game board opens (see Figure 20-7). Click a square on the board, and a timer starts counting the seconds of your game.

   - If you click a square and a number appears, the number tells you how many mines are within the eight squares surrounding that square; if it remains blank, there are no mines within the eight squares surrounding it.

   - If you click a square and a bomb appears, all the hidden bombs are exposed (see Figure 20-8), and the game is over.

   - Right-click a square once to place a flag on it marking it as a mine. Right-click a square twice to place a question mark on it if you think it might contain a bomb to warn yourself to stay away for now.

3. To begin a new game, choose Game⇨New Game. In the New Game dialog box, click Quit and Start a New Game. If you want to play a game with the same settings as the previous one, click Restart This Game.

4. You can set several game options through the Game menu:

   - To change the expertise required, choose Game⇨ Options and then choose Beginner, Intermediate, or Advanced.

   - To change the color of the playing board choose Game⇨Change Appearance.

   - If you want to see how many games you've won, your longest winning or losing streak and more, choose Game⇨Statistics.

5. To end the game, click the Close button.

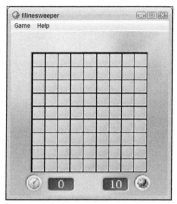

Figure 20-7: A new Minesweeper game

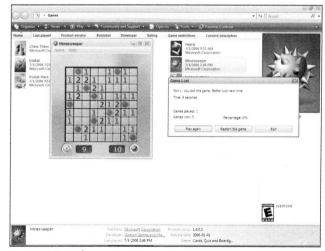

Figure 20-8: You lose!

 If you want a bigger game board (more squares, more bombs, more fun) choose Game⇨Options and then click Custom and specify the number of squares across, down, and the number of bombs hidden within them.

Play Purble Place

1. Choose Start⮞Games; double-click Purble Place.

    Purble Place is actually made up of three games: Comfy Cakes, Purble Shop, and Purble Pairs. All are aimed at younger children to help them learn to match things, and all offer easy to follow pop-up instructions.

2. In the resulting Purble Place window (see Figure 20-9), click one of three items to begin a game:

   - The schoolhouse opens Purble Pairs, where you click two squares at a time, trying to find pairs of items.

   - The bakery displays Comfy Cakes, where you assemble a cake to match the picture.

   - The Purble Shop contains a little character for whom you have to select eyes, nose, and mouth that match.

3. In the game window (Figure 20-10 shows Comfy Cakes), follow the onscreen instructions to make selections. In Comfy Cakes, for example, click a cake shape and then click the large green arrow button on the screen to move the cake to the next station. Choose icing and decorations that match the picture of the cake on the TV.

4. To return to the main menu, choose Game⮞Main Menu. To exit the game entirely, click the Close button.

    There's a shortcut in each game window to get back to the main menu. Click the little building icons (shop, school, and home) that are surrounded by a green arrow.

Figure 20-9: The Purble Place main menu

Figure 20-10: The Comfy Cakes game

Play Hearts

1. Choose Start⇨Games and double-click Hearts. If you've never played before, you'll see a Microsoft Hearts Network dialog box; enter your name and click OK.

2. In the resulting Hearts window, as shown in Figure 20-11, your hand is displayed while others are hidden. Begin play by clicking three cards to pass to your opponent, and then clicking the Pass Left button.

3. Each player moving clockwise around the window plays a card of the same suit by clicking it. The one who plays the highest card of the suit in play wins the trick. (A *trick* is the cards you collect when you play the highest card of the suit.)

4. Choose Game⇨Options to change the settings shown in Figure 20-12. You can rename the other three players, play sounds, show tips, or specify how to save a game.

5. To end the game, choose Game⇨Exit or click the Close button.

 Check out the menus in the Games window for organizing and customizing the various games that Windows Vista makes available and to set Parental Controls.

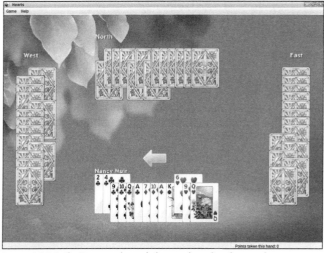

Figure 20-11: The Hearts window with three cards ready to be passed

Figure 20-12: The Hearts Options dialog box

Add a USB Joystick to Your Computer

1. To connect a USB joystick or other type of game controller, simply plug it into a USB port on your computer. Connect to a game port by plugging the device into the port you want to use on your computer. Windows Vista should recognize it and install it automatically.

2. If your device isn't recognized automatically, continue with the following steps.

3. Choose Start⇨Games⇨Tools⇨Input Devices.

4. In the resulting Game Controllers dialog box, as shown in Figure 20-13, click Add.

5. In the resulting list of controllers (see Figure 20-14), click the one that you plugged in and then click OK twice.

 If your device controller isn't listed in the Game Controller dialog box, insert the installation disk/c that came with it and follow directions to install it. If you don't have an installation disk/c, either the device manual or the manufacturer's Web site might indicate that there's a compatible driver that's already installed with Windows that you could use, so follow Step 5 to select that driver. Alternatively, you can click the Custom button, make selections there, and let Windows select a likely driver. One final option: The manufacturer might offer a downloadable version of the driver on its Web site.

Figure 20-13: The Game Controllers dialog box

Figure 20-14: The list of available game controllers

Playing Music in Windows Vista

Chapter

21

W ho doesn't love music? It sets our toes tapping and puts a song in our hearts. It's the perfect accompaniment to spice up the drudgery of working on a computer for hours on end, so wouldn't it be great if you could play music right at your desk without having to take up valuable desktop space with a CD player or even an iPod?

Good news: You might not realize it, but your Windows Vista computer is a lean, mean, music machine. With a sound card installed and speakers attached, it's a hi-tech desktop boombox that can play sound files and CD/DVDs. Using Windows media programs, you can create playlists and even burn music tracks to a CD/DVD or sync to your portable device to download music to it.

The ins and outs of music on your computer, which you discover in this chapter, include

- ➡ Getting your computer ready for listening by setting up your speakers and adjusting the volume.

- ➡ Downloading music from the Internet or a CD/DVD and playing it.

- ➡ Managing your music by creating playlists of tracks you download.

- ➡ Burning tracks to CD/DVD or syncing to download music to portable devices so you and your music can hit the road.

Get ready to . . .

Set Up Speakers

1. Attach speakers to your computer by plugging them into the appropriate connection (often labeled with a little megaphone or speaker symbol) on your CPU, laptop, or monitor.

2. Choose Start⇨Control Panel⇨Hardware and Sound; then click the Manage Audio Devices link (under Sound).

3. In the resulting Audio Devices dialog box (see Figure 21-1), double-click the Speakers item.

4. In the resulting Speakers dialog box, click the Levels tab, as shown in Figure 21-2, and then use the Speakers slider to adjust the speaker volume. *Note:* If there is a small red x on the speaker button, click it to activate the speakers.

5. Click the Balance button. In the resulting Balance dialog box, use the L(eft) and R(ight) sliders to adjust the balance of sounds between the two speakers.

6. Click OK three times to close all the open dialog boxes and save the new settings.

 You can test your speakers. On the Advanced tab of the Speakers dialog box, choose your speaker configuration and then click the Test button. This tests first one speaker and then the other to help you pinpoint whether one of your speakers is having problems or whether you should adjust the balance between the speakers for better sound.

Figure 21-1: The Audio Devices dialog box

Figure 21-2: The Speakers dialog box

Adjust Volume

1. Choose Start⇨Control Panel⇨Hardware and Sound.

2. Click the Adjust System Volume link under Sound to display the Volume dialog box (as shown in Figure 21-3).

3. Make any of the following settings:

   • Move the Device volume slider to adjust the main system volume up and down.

   • For sounds played by Windows, adjust the volume by moving the Applications slider.

   • To mute either main or application volume, click the speaker icon beneath either slider so that a red symbol appears.

4. Click the Close button twice.

 Here's a handy shortcut for quickly adjusting the volume of your default sound device. Click the Volume button (which looks like a little gray speaker) in the System Tray. To adjust the volume, use the slider on the Volume pop-up that appears, or select the Mute check box to turn off sounds temporarily.

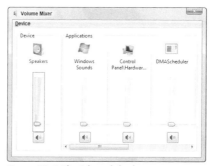

Figure 21-3: The Volume dialog box

 Today many keyboards include volume controls and a mute button to control sounds from your computer. Some even include buttons to play, pause, and stop audio playback. Having these buttons and other controls at your fingertips can be worth a little extra in the price of your keyboard.

Create a Playlist

1. Choose Start⇨All Programs⇨Windows Media Player.

2. Click the Library tab and then click Create Playlist at the left under the Playlists item. The Create Playlist label disappears, and a text box opens in its place; enter a playlist title there and then click outside it. A blank playlist appears in the List pane on the right.

3. Click a library in the left pane of the Media Library, and the library contents appear (see Figure 21-4). Click an item and then drag it to the new playlist. Repeat this step to locate additional titles to add to the playlist.

4. When you finish adding titles, click Save Playlist. To play a playlist, click it in the Library pane and then click the Play button.

5. You can manage the list by right-clicking it and choosing Edit in List Pane. Click the arrow next to the playlist title and use the drop-down menu commands (see Figure 21-5) to do tasks, such as

   • Choose Sort to sort the playlist by title, artists, release date, and so on.

   • Choose Shuffle List Now to randomly reorganize the titles to play in a different order.

   • Choose Rename Playlist to give it a different name.

   • Choose Skipped Items to indicate how to deal with tracks you have skipped.

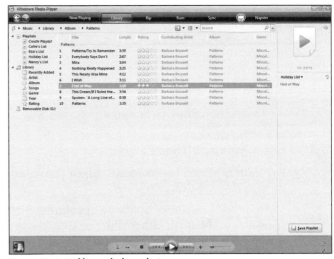

Figure 21-4: Building a playlist in the List pane

Figure 21-5: The menu for editing a playlist

 You can also right-click a playlist in the Library pane and choose Play to play it or choose Delete to delete the list, though the original tracks that make up the list still exist.

Burn Music to a CD/DVD

1. Insert a blank CD or DVD suitable for storing audio files in your computer CD/DVD-RW drive.

2. Open the Windows Media Player, click the Library or Burn button, and then click one more albums or playlists to play and drag them to the Burn pane (see Figure 21-6).

3. Click Start Burn. Windows Media Player begins to burn the items to the disc. The Status column for the first song title reads `Writing to Disc` and changes to `Complete` when the track is copied.

4. When the burn is complete, your disc is ejected (although you can change this option by choosing Burn⇨Eject Disc After Burning to deselect it).

If you swap music online through various music-sharing services and then copy them to CD/DVD and pass them around to your friends, always do a virus check on the files before handing them off. Also, be sure you have the legal right to download and swap music with others.

Note that DVDs come in different types, including DVD+, DVD- and DVD+/-. You must be sure your DVD drive is compatible with the disc type you are using or you cannot burn the DVD successfully. Check the packaging for the format before you buy!

Figure 21-6: Music displayed in the Burn pane waiting to be copied

Rip Music from a CD/DVD

1. Insert an audio CD/DVD in your computer's CD/DVD-RW drive.

2. Open the Windows Media Player, click the Library tab, and then click an album or playlist to open it.

3. Click the Rip tab. The titles on the currently open item are automatically *ripped* (copied) to the open library. If there is a track you don't want to copy, mark its check box in the Rip window (see Figure 21-7).

4. When the rip is complete, the titles appear in the playlist in the Library window.

 You can click the arrow on the Rip tab button to view a menu of options. By using this, you can modify when a rip occurs (when in the Rip tab, never, or always), the format and bit rate, and whether to eject the CD/DVD after ripping.

 Windows Media Player offers a few different formats for ripping. For example, Windows Media Audio offers you a smaller file size and good audio quality. Windows Media Audio Lossless provides better quality at the cost of a larger file size. Other choices include MP3 and WAV. To change this setting click the arrow under the Rip button and choose Format and click on an option in the menu that appears.

Figure 21-7: A playlist displayed in the List pane

Play Music

1. Choose Start➪All Programs➪Accessories➪Windows Media Player.

2. Click the Library tab to display the library shown in Figure 21-8. Click an album or playlist to open it; the titles of the songs are displayed in the right pane.

3. Use the buttons on the bottom of the Player window (as shown in Figure 21-9) to do the following:

   • Click a track, and then click the Play button to play it.

   • Click the Stop button to stop playback.

   • Click the Next or Previous button to move to the next or previous track in an album or playlist.

   • Use the Mute and Volume controls to pump the sound up or down without having to modify the Windows volume settings.

 Tired of the order in which your tracks play? You can use the Turn Shuffle On button on the far left of the playback controls to have Windows Media Player move around the tracks on your album randomly. Click this button again to turn the shuffle feature off.

 To jump to another track, rather than using the Next and Previous buttons you can click a track in the track list in the Media Player window. This can be much quicker if you want to jump several tracks ahead or behind of the currently playing track.

Figure 21-8: A selected album or playlist

Figure 21-9: The playback tools

Set Up Your Default Online Stores

1. Choose Start⇨All Programs⇨Accessories⇨Windows Media Player.

2. Choose Online Stores⇨Browse All Online Stores. *Note:* If you've set up a default online store, the Online Stores button displays that store's name.

3. In the resulting window displaying a choice of online stores (see Figure 21-10), click a category in the list on the left and then click a store. A message appears confirming that you want to go to this store. Click Yes. This store is now your default store in this category, and its name is displayed on the Online Stores button.

4. In the resulting store Web site, follow that site's procedure to browse or make purchases.

5. When you finish shopping, click any of the tabs in Media Player to close the online store and return to using Media Player.

 If you've set up a store in more than one category, whichever store you visited last is displayed on the Online Stores button. To easily switch to another store, click the arrow on the Online Stores button and choose Add Current Service to Menu. Now you can quickly go to that store by choosing it from the menu.

 To display a media guide that covers movies, music, radio stations, and even cartoons, click the arrow on the Online Stores button and choose Media Guide. This takes you to `www.windows media.com`, with news, links, free skins, device reviews, and more.

Figure 21-10: A variety of stores to choose from

Sync to a Portable Device

1. Open Windows Media Player and connect your device to your computer.

2. A Sync List pane appears on the right. Click and drag items in your library you want to sync to your device into the Sync pane (see Figure 21-11).

3. Click Start Sync. The Sync status shows in Media Player. When it's done, all items will show as Synchronized to Device (see Figure 21-12).

 To sync to another connected device, just click the Next Device link in the Sync pane, build your sync list by clicking and dragging items to the pane, and click Start Sync again.

If you have trouble syncing to your device, be sure to check the device user manual. With new types of devices coming out all the time, some may be configured differently and need to be set up to work with your computer and Windows Vista.

Figure 21-11: The Sync List pane

Figure 21-12: Windows Media Player in the process of syncing to a device

Working with Photos in Photo Gallery

Chapter 22

A picture is worth a thousand words, and that's probably why everybody is in on the digital image craze. Most people today have access to a digital camera (even if only on their cellphones) and have started manipulating and swapping photos like crazy, both online and off.

Although Chapter 4 gives you a quick peek at how to view images in the Photo Gallery, there's much more to this feature of Windows Vista than that. In this chapter, you discover how to

➟ View your photos and run a slide show of them.

➟ Work with tags to help you organize and search through photos.

➟ E-mail a photo to others or burn photos to a CD or DVD to pass around to your friends.

➟ Fix a photo by adjusting its exposure or color, or cropping it to focus on the part of the image you like best.

Get ready to . . .

View a Digital Image in the Windows Photo Gallery

1. Choose Start⇨All Programs⇨Windows Photo Gallery.

2. In the resulting Windows Photo Gallery window, as shown in Figure 22-1, click any of the items in the Navigation pane on the left to choose which images to display (such as those taken in a certain year or saved in a certain folder).

3. Double-click an image to display it. Then you can use the tools at the bottom of the window (see Figure 22-2) to do any of the following:

    *   The **Next** and **Previous** icons move to a previous or following image in the same folder.

    *   The **Display Size** icon displays a slider you can click and drag to change the size of the image thumbnails.

    *   The **Delete** button deletes the selected image.

    *   The **Rotate Clockwise** and **Rotate Counterclockwise** icons spin the image 90 degrees at a time.

4. When you finish viewing images, click the Close button in the top-right corner to close the Photo Gallery.

 If you add additional photos to the Photo Gallery, click the arrow on the Choose a Thumbnail View (to the left of the Search box) and choose Refresh. All photos will be reshuffled into applicable categories.

Figure 22-1: The Windows Photo Gallery

Figure 22-2: The tools you can use to manipulate images

Add a Tag to a Photo

1. To create a new tag, click the Create a New Tag item in the Navigation pane. The box opens for editing. Type a tag name and then click anywhere outside it.

2. Click a file to select it.

3. Click the Info button. All tags associated with the photo appear on the right of the gallery window (see Figure 22-3).

4. Click Add Tags, begin to type a tag name, and choose it from the drop-down list that appears (see Figure 22-4). Press Enter to add the tag, which then appears in the list of tags associated with that photo.

5. To see all photos associated with a certain tag, click the tag in the Tags list in the Navigation pane.

 To delete a tag, right-click the tag in the Navigation pane and choose Delete. To rename a tag, right-click it and choose Rename.

 To see a list of all photos in the Photo Gallery organized by tags, click the Tags item in Navigation pane. Categories appear in the Photo Gallery window with a note of the total items with that associated tag.

Figure 22-3: Information about a photo's associated tags

Figure 22-4: Adding a tag to a photo

Organize Photos by Date

1. Click a month or date in the Date Taken section of Navigation pane. Photos taken in that timeframe are displayed (see Figure 22-5).

2. Right-click a photo and choose Properties.

3. On the Details tab of the Properties dialog box that appears (see Figure 22-6), click the Date Taken field and adjust the date by typing a new one, or click the calendar icon and choose a new date from the pop-up calendar.

4. Click OK. The photo is now in the newly selected date's folder.

Figure 22-5: The contents of a Date Taken folder

 Another way to organize photos is to rate them by whatever criteria you want. When you assign a rating to your photos, you can then view them by using the Ratings category in the list on the left. To add a rating to a photo, select it and then click the Info button. Click the chosen star for the rating number; that is, if you want to rate a photo a 3, click the third star from the left.

 You can also change other properties of a photo or video in the Properties dialog box. For example, you can change the title, subject, rating, author, date acquired, and copyright. If you're serious about your photography, you can even add information about camera make, model, lenses, and aperture settings here.

Figure 22-6: The Properties dialog box

Play a Slide Show

1. With the Photo Gallery open, click the set of slides you'd like to use for the slide show from the Navigation pane.

2. Click the Play Slide Show button, as shown in Figure 22-7. The slide show begins to play.

3. Slides proceed at a preset speed. You can change this speed by right-clicking your screen and choosing Slide Show Speed Slow, Medium, or Fast (see Figure 22-8).

4. To move more quickly to the next or previous slide, press the right- or left-arrow key on your keyboard.

5. To pause the show, right-click and choose Pause.

6. To end the show, press Esc on your keyboard.

 If you want to create a custom show, you can create a new tag, assign it to the photos you want to be in the show, and then choose that tag in the Navigation pane before running the show. See the earlier task, "Add a Tag to a Photo," for more about how to do this.

Figure 22-7: Choosing the slides to include in your show

Figure 22-8: The shortcut menu for controlling a show in progress

E-Mail a Photo

1. With the Photo Gallery open and the item you want to e-mail selected, click the E-mail button.

2. In the Attach Files dialog box that appears (see Figure 22-9), change the photo size by clicking the Picture Size drop-down arrow and choosing another size from the list.

3. Click Attach. An e-mail form from your default e-mail application appears with your photo attached (see Figure 22-10).

4. Fill out the e-mail form with an addressee, subject, and message (if you wish), and then click Send.

 Choose smaller size photos to attach to an e-mail because graphic files can be rather big. You might encounter problems sending larger files, or others might have trouble receiving them. Using a smaller size is especially important if you are sending multiple images. Note that although you can send a video file as an e-mail attachment, you can't resize it; video files make photo files look tiny by comparison, so it's probably better to send one at a time, if at all.

 You can also open an e-mail form first. Then, with the Photo Gallery open, click and drag a photo to your e-mail. This method attaches the original file size to the message.

Figure 22-9: The Attach Files dialog box

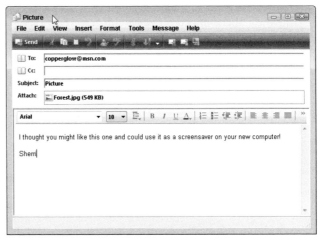

Figure 22-10: An e-mail message with an image attached

Fix a Photo

1. With the Photo Gallery open, display a photo by locating it with the Navigation pane; then click the thumbnail to select it.

2. Click the Fix button. The Fix window appears, as shown in Figure 22-11. Click Auto Adjust to let Photo Gallery fix the photo, or use any of these tools (click the tool name once to display options and click it again to close that tool):

   - Click **Adjust Exposure** and use the sliders to adjust brightness and contrast.

   - Click **Adjust Color** and use the sliders (see Figure 22-12) to adjust temperature, tint, and saturation.

   - Click **Crop Picture** and use the handles on the rectangle that appears to enlarge or shrink the area on the photo to be cropped, or click the rectangle and drag it around your picture to crop to another location on it. Click the Apply button to apply the cropping. When you click the Apply button, it applies and saves the change.

   - If your picture contains a face with red, glowing eyes, click the **Fix Red Eye** tool and then click and drag around the eye you want to fix in your image to adjust it.

3. You can use the navigation tools at the bottom to zoom in or out, fit the image to the window, move to the next image, undo or redo actions, or delete the picture. When you're finished, click the Back to Gallery button.

 The Undo feature in this window allows you to pick the action you want to undo, unlike many Undo features that force you to undo all the actions leading back to the action you want to undo. Click the arrow on the Undo item under the tools, rather than on the set of buttons along the bottom, to use this feature.

Figure 22-11: The Fix window

Figure 22-12: The Adjust Color tools

Burn a Photo to a CD or DVD

1. Insert a writable CD or DVD disc into your disc drive.

2. With the Photo Gallery open, display a photo by locating it with the Navigation pane and then clicking the thumbnail to select it. To select additional images, hold Ctrl while clicking additional images.

3. Click the Burn button and then choose Data Disc.

4. In the resulting Burn a Disc dialog box (see Figure 22-13), enter a disc title and click then Next to accept the Mastered format, which is readable on most computers.

5. In the Windows Explorer window that appears for your disc drive (see Figure 22-14), click the Burn to Disc button to proceed.

6. The Burn a Disc window appears. If you wish, modify the disc title or adjust the recording speed and then click Next. A progress bar appears.

7. When the files have been burned to the disc, a confirming dialog box appears, and your disc drawer opens. Click Finish to complete the process and close the wizard.

 In the confirmation dialog box that appears in Step 6, you can select the Yes, Burn These Files to Another Disc check box if you want to make another copy of the same files.

Figure 22-13: The Burn a Disc dialog box

Figure 22-14: Images ready to be burned to a disc

Index

• H •

• I •

• J •

• K •

• L •

• M •